D1355891

Payment Card Industry Data Security Standard Handbook

Timothy M. Virtue

WILEY

John Wiley & Sons, Inc.

Published by John Wiley & Sons, Inc., Hoboken, New Jersey.
Published simultaneously in Canada.

Portions of this text are reprinted with permission from "Payment Card Industry (PCI) Data
Security Standard, Version 1.1 (Release: September 2006)", the contemporaneous version
of which is available at the following internet address: https://www.pcisecuritystandards
.org/pdfs/pci_dss_v1-1.pdf and "Payment Card Industry (PCI) Data Security Standard:
Glossary, Abbreviations and Acronyms", the contemporaneous version of which is
available at the following internet address: https://www.pcisecuritystandards
.org/pdfs/pci_dss_glossary_v1-1.pdf.

For general information on our other products and services, or technical support, please
contact our Customer Care Department within the United States at 800-762-2974, outside the
United States at 317-572-3993 or fax 317-572-4002.

Wiley also publishes its books in a variety of electronic formats. Some content that appears in
print may not be available in electronic books.

For more information about Wiley products, visit our Web site at *www.wiley.com*.

Library of Congress Cataloging-in-Publication Data:

Virtue, Timothy M., 1975-
    Payment card industry data security standard handbook / Timothy M. Virtue.
        p.   cm.
    Includes bibliographical references and index.
    ISBN 978-0-470-26046-3 (cloth)
        1. Credit cards—Security measures.   2. Data protection.   I. Title.
    HG3755.7.V57   2009
    332.1'788028558—dc22

                                                                    2008023247

Printed in the United States of America

10 9 8 7 6 5 4 3 2 1

This book is dedicated to my loving wife, Courtney.
Thank you for all of the love, support, and inspiration
you provided on this project and through all of life.

I would also like to thank my many wonderful
family members, friends, teachers, and colleagues who
have contributed to my growth and success over the years.

CONTENTS

Chapter

INTRODUCTION

This text is intended to guide, mentor, and otherwise assist organizations along their journey to compliance with the Payment Card Industry Data Security Standard (PCI DSS). Organizations that want to become PCI DSS compliant will find that many aspects of the program offer relatively little flexibility. After all, we are discussing compliance with industry imposed regulations, not a set of suggested best practices. However, several of the requirements can be achieved in many different fashions (within reason, and assuming the intent of the requirement is satisfied). I felt the best approach to addressing such a broad and complex compliance initiative was to create a text that could be used as an initial primer on PCI compliance and be referenced to support an organization's maintenance of an ongoing commitment to PCI compliance, and to offer suggested strategies and detailed references that can be used to expand upon concepts discussed in this text.

The specific approach I took to achieve these goals was to break down the information into individually sustainable parts that can be read one after the other or else referenced individually. The text is divided into three parts: "The Fundamentals," "PCI Breakdown," and "Strategy and Operations." Part One, "The Fundamentals," addresses foundational information security practices. This part offers the benefit of an information security primer for those who have less of a background in the subject. It also provides an overall view of the essential components and best practices of a successful information security program. This understanding is critical to achieving PCI DSS compliance, since many of the PCI DSS requirements are based on industry best practices and a comprehensive information security program.

Part Two, "PCI Breakdown," is the heart of the book. It sequentially lists all of the PCI DSS requirements and provides brief explanations, clarifications, or recommendations as applicable. Depending on the specific PCI DSS requirement, the level of detail of the additional information varies. Some of the requirements are very clear and address relatively straightforward topics, while others deal with concerns that are very complex and ordinarily take years to master. Indeed, some of these topics can take up entire books. I have attempted to strike a balance between offering the minimum required knowledge and providing a comprehensive discussion.

Part Three, "Strategy and Operations," offers information that organizations can utilize to achieve and maintain ongoing compliance with PCI DSS. Compliance is not a onetime event or a checked box on an audit form. Organizations will need to remain proactive in their compliance efforts. They will need to remain abreast of both external and internal influences on their organization. Since changes will inevitably occur with PCI DSS requirements, technology, consumer demands, regulatory/legal requirements, and the business environment, organizations must adapt to protect the cardholder data environment while maintaining business objectives.

For those seeking higher levels of knowledge, I have also included a Resources section. This section will address situations where readers may need a more comprehensive discussion of the subject.

Since every organization is different and complex technology environments need to be managed on a case-by-case basis, I would encourage readers to leverage this text to embrace the requirements of PCI DSS compliance and adapt them accordingly to suit your organization's specific needs. It is important to note that because of the ever-changing technology and business environment facing today's organizations, PCI DSS compliance must be viewed as a cyclical and long-term process.

Finally, I wish each of you much success in your journey to achieving PCI DSS compliance for your organization.

PART 1

The Fundamentals

CHAPTER 1

PCI Fundamentals

The Payment Card Industry Data Security Standards (PCI DSS) is commonly referred to as *PCI compliance*. Although this is one of the hottest topics of discussion among business and technology professionals alike, the spirit of PCI compliance is nothing new. In fact it has been around for several years. However, with the rise of information security–related legislation, privacy concerns, confirmed data breaches, and the overall prevalence of e-commerce in today's society, PCI compliance is of the utmost concern for a wide assortment of people, organizations, and businesses.

Although the rise of e-commerce has had a profound economic impact on our daily lives at both the personal and professional levels, it brings a host of new challenges, including the challenge of properly protecting sensitive cardholder data. In all business activities, a certain amount of risk is assumed in order to gain the benefits associated with that business activity. In the world of payment cards and electronic commerce, the risk-and-reward model involves properly protecting cardholder data during payment card transactions. The importance of protecting cardholder data can't be overstated.

Many of the key players in the payment card industry got together to develop a series of best practices that could be implemented by those utilizing payment cards. In today's world of new legislation, regulation, and compliance, the payment card industry sought to develop a program where the industry could be self-regulated and proactively manage the risks associated with payment card programs. The goal of this initiative was to reduce governmental legislation and build confidence and trust among the participants (including consumers) that rely on payment cards to conduct commerce.

PCI compliance is important for a number of reasons, and no single reason outweighs any other. Their combined weight is what drives us toward compliance. Each reason falls under one of two headings: consumer confidence or effective business operations. From a consumer perspective, it is all about confidence. Consumers place enormous trust in those who use their sensitive cardholder data as part of their daily commerce. Although a majority of us take advantage of the convenience and efficiency associated with today's electronic commerce, we do so with the expectation that our transactions will be performed in a secure manner. In a world of significant choice, consumers can easily select other vendors to provide their services if they are not comfortable in the security of their personal information. From a business perspective, organizations want to transact commerce in a secure manner so that they can maintain their customer's confidence, have reduced operational costs, and protect organizational assets from fraud and abuse. On a larger scale, our economy depends on efficient trade markets. When commerce can be conducted electronically, there are tremendous gains in efficiency and globalization. When these daily operations are threatened by potential fraud and abuse, businesses are at risk of not being able to effectively operate in today's e-commerce–based markets. The importance of these factors led to the establishment of the PCI and the corresponding data security standards.

There are numerous specific measures organizations can take to create a secure operating environment for the processing of payment cards. The PCI Security Standards Council has established 12 detailed control objectives, which are grouped into 6 broader categories:

1. Build and maintain a secure network.
2. Protect cardholder data.

3. Maintain a vulnerability management program.
4. Implement strong access control measures.
5. Regularly monitor and test networks.
6. Maintain an information security policy.

These six categories are the critical foundation for creating, protecting, maintaining, and operating in a secure manner.

HISTORY OF PCI

The PCI DSS is a standard that has evolved over many years by the efforts of the major payment card brands. Prior to PCI DSS, the major payment card brands individually developed various standards to improve the security of sensitive information used by the payment card industry. Visa USA had originally launched the Cardholder Information Security Program (CISP) in June 2001. From then until March 2004, these audit procedures underwent several revisions and continued to grow and evolve to address the many facets of protecting sensitive cardholder data.

There was also early collaboration between MasterCard and Visa in an attempt to validate and protect cardholder data. During these early attempts at collaboration, some gaps and inconsistency occurred between the separate programs. Although well intentioned, the relationship had a number of problems. The list of approved vendors was not well maintained and there was no clear way for security vendors to get added to the list. Another significant problem was that the other major payment card brands, such as Discover, American Express, and JCB (Japan Credit Bureau), were running their own programs and there was little collaboration across the entire industry.

This lack of collaboration caused tremendous hardships for merchants and service providers, as many of them spent a significant amount of resources to comply with the individual security programs offered by all of the major payment card brands. In order to overcome the challenges and offer a comprehensive information security program for the payment card industry, all of the major brands worked together and developed PCI DSS 1.0. To further solidify the ownership of the standards, the PCI Security Standards Council was founded. The council maintains the ownership of the PCI DSS, the approved vendor lists, training programs, and other relevant program details.

Although the primary focus of this text is compliance with PCI DSS, it should also be noted that each payment card brand also maintains its own security program in addition to the PCI DSS. These programs go beyond the data protection charter of PCI and include activities such as fraud prevention. The details of such programs can be found in the Resources section of this text. It is highly recommended that organizations adopt the specific card brand recommendations (as applicable to your organization) in addition to PCI DSS to further strengthen their overall security posture.

At the time of this writing, the PCI organization is in its early stages and evolving, and it will continue to grow and improve over time. Inevitably, this maturation process will strengthen the council's ability to deliver security-minded services to merchants and service providers. Due to this fact, it is recommended that organizations continuously monitor and consult the PCI Council's resources and Web site (pcisecuritystandards.org) on a regular basis to ensure that appropriate levels of compliance are achieved and maintained by your organization.

WHY PCI DSS?

The short answer is because it is required. Fortunately, there are many additional benefits to achieving PCI DSS compliance. Fundamentally, many of the methodologies and specific requirements associated with PCI DSS are actually industry standards or best practices. Any organization that can implement and manage the components of PCI DSS will significantly improve its overall security posture and fortify its protection of sensitive cardholder data. Also, PCI DSS compliance offers many organizational benefits and specific risk mitigation solutions.

The cardholder data environment has an aggregated risk based on the subrisk categories of *reputation, financial, compliance,* and *operational.* Exhibit 1.1 represents how each category of risk is tied together to create an overall level of risk for the cardholder data environment.

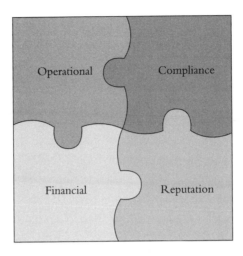

EXHIBIT 1.1   Aggregated Risk for Cardholder Data Environment

Risk	Example
Reputation	What is the impact of a PCI DSS compliance violation on your institution's brand?
Financial	• The fines from specific credit card issuers (i.e., Visa, MasterCard, and American Express) • Litigation costs associated with security breach • Merchant banks will receive fines as a result of a security breach.
Compliance	• Risk of noncompliance with PCI DSS • The fines from specific credit card issuers (i.e., Visa, MasterCard, and American Express)
Operational	• Credit card company–imposed operating restrictions • Loss of card processing privileges

EXHIBIT 1.2   Examples of Cardholder Data Environment Risk

Exhibit 1.2 provides examples of the risks that organizations face within their cardholder data environment.

Furthermore, the direct costs associated with a data breach are significantly increasing on an annual basis. In fact, research from the

Ponemon Institute has shown that the cost of a data breach continues to rise and has done so by 43 percent since 2005. Highlights from the institute's *2007 Annual Study: U.S. Cost of a Data Breach* follow:

- **Total costs increase.** The total average costs of a data breach grew to $197 per record compromised, an increase of 8 percent since 2006 and 43 percent compared with 2005. The average total cost per reporting company was more than $6.3 million per breach and ranged from $225,000 to almost $35 million.
- **Cost of lost business accelerates.** The cost of lost business continued to increase at more than 30 percent, averaging $4.1 million, or $128 per record compromised. Lost business now accounts for 65 percent of data breach costs compared with 54 percent in the 2006 study.
- **Third-party data breaches increase, and cost more.** Breaches by third-party organizations such as outsourcers, contractors, consultants, and business partners were reported by 40 percent of respondents, up from 29 percent in 2006 and 21 percent in 2005. Breaches by third parties were also more costly than breaches by the enterprise itself, averaging $231 compared with $171 per record.
- **Increased customer churn rates help drive lost business costs higher.** In 2007, the average resulting abnormal customer churn rate was 2.67 percent, an increase from 2.01 percent in 2006. Greater customer turnover leads to lower revenues and a higher cost of new customer acquisition resulting from increased marketing to recover lost customer business.
- **Legal defense, public relations costs increase.** Indicating continued growing dissatisfaction and action over a data breach, the costs that organizations expended for legal defense and public relations grew to 8 percent and 3 percent of total breach costs, respectively.
- **Financial services firms impacted most.** The cost of a data breach for financial services organizations was $239 per compromised record, or more than 21 percent higher than the average, demonstrating that organizations with high expectations of trust and privacy have more to lose from a data breach.

The Ponemon Institute research clearly demonstrates the costs associated with a data security breach. Since most organizations are not likely to want to absorb these additional costs, we can clearly see the financial benefits of protecting the cardholder data environment and embracing PCI DSS to reduce the likelihood of a data breach. Now that we have an understanding of what exactly drives PCI DSS, we can begin to discuss what it is and what it means to your organization.

A fundamental component of PCI DSS compliance is to understand the terms, definitions, and requirements put fourth by the PCI Security Standards Council. Throughout this text, I will be referring to the terms and definitions that are listed in the Payment Card Industry Data Security Standards Glossary, Abbreviations, and Acronyms document. In Exhibits 1.3, 1.4, and 1.5, I have included selected terms in order to clarify key components of the PCI Data Security Standard. It is strongly recommended that you frequently review the glossary, abbreviations, and acronyms documentation on a regular basis for any updates or modifications. In addition, this document is an invaluable resource for a more detailed understanding of relevant PCI DSS terms and definitions. The link to the complete list is located in the Resources section of this text.

Now that we have an understanding of key payment card industry terms and definitions, we can review a typical payment card transaction. Exhibit 1.6 illustrates a typical payment card transaction:

The following three steps explain a typical payment card transaction and highlight the associated parties required to complete the transaction:

Step 1. A cardholder is made an authorized user of a payment card by the card issuer (a financial institution that issues the card based on predetermined repayment terms).

Step 2. The authorized card user then initiates a transaction with a merchant (an authorized acceptor of the payment card who receives payment for goods and services).

Step 3. The merchant processes the transaction with an acquirer, referred to as a *merchant bank*. This is a financial institution under contract with the card brand to accept and process the payment.

Term	Definition
Account Number	Payment card number (credit or debit) that identifies the issuer and the particular cardholder account. Also called Primary Account Number (PAN).
Cardholder	Customer to whom a card is issued or an individual who is authorized to use the card.
Cardholder Data	Full magnetic stripe or the PAN plus any of the following: ✓ Cardholder Name ✓ Expiration Date ✓ Service Code
Card Validation Value or Code	Data element on a card's magnetic stripe that uses secure cryptographic process to protect its data integrity and to reveal any alteration or counterfeiting. Also referred to as CAV, CVC, CVV, or CSC, depending on the payment card brand. *Note: The second type of card validation value or code is the three-digit value printed to the right of the credit card number in the signature panel area on the back of the card. For American Express cards, the code is a four-digit unembossed number printed above the card number on the face of all payment cards. The code is uniquely associated with each individual piece of plastic and ties the card account number to the plastic.*

EXHIBIT 1.3 Card-Specific Information

Term	Definition
Hosting Provider	Offers various services to merchants and other service providers. Services range from simple to complex: from shared space on a server to a whole range of "shopping cart" options; from payment applications to connections to payment gateways and processors; and hosting dedicated to just one customer per server.
Magnetic Stripe Data (Track Data)	Data encoded in the magnetic stripe used for authorization during transactions when the card is presented. Entities must not retain full magnetic stripe data subsequent to transaction authorization. Specifically, subsequent to authorization, service codes, discretionary data/Card Validation Value/Code (CVV), and proprietary reserved values must be purged; however, account number, expiration date, name, and service code may be extracted and retained, if needed for business.
Payment Cardholder Environment	That part of the network that possesses cardholder data or sensitive authentication data.
PIN	Personal Identification Number
POS	Point of Sale
PVV	PIN Verification Value. This is encoded in the magnetic stripe of a payment card.
Sensitive Authentication Data	Security-related information (Card Validation Codes/Values, complete track data, PINs, and PIN Blocks) used to authenticate cardholders, appearing in plaintext or otherwise unprotected form. Disclosure, modification, or destruction of this information could compromise the security of a cryptographic device, information system, or cardholder information or could be used in a fraudulent transaction.

EXHIBIT 1.4   Transaction-Specific Information

Term	Definition
Acquirer	The bankcard association member that initiates and maintains relationships with merchants that accept payment cards. (Also referred to as merchant bank.)
Cardholder Data Environment	The area of a computer system network that possesses cardholder data or sensitive authentication data, and those systems and segments that directly attach or support cardholder processing, storage, or transmission. Adequate network segmentation, which isolates systems that store, process, or transmit cardholder data from those that do not, may reduce the scope of the cardholder data environment and thus the scope of the PCI assessment.
Issuer	The financial institution that issues a payment card.
Merchant	Any company that accepts payment cards in exchange for goods or services.
Service Provider	A business entity that is not a payment card brand member or a merchant directly involved in the processing, storage, transmission, and switching of transaction data and cardholder information or both. This also includes companies that provide services to merchants, service providers, or members that control or could impact the security of cardholder data. Examples include managed service providers that provide managed firewalls, IDS, and other services, as well as hosting providers and other entities. Entities such as telecommunications companies that only provide communication links without access to the application layer of the communication link are excluded.

EXHIBIT 1.5   Organization-Specific Information

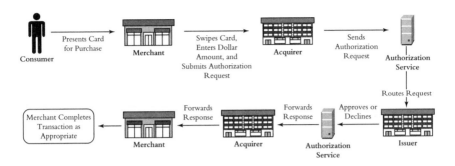

EXHIBIT 1.6   Typical Payment Card Transaction

Each payment card brand has defined a set of merchant levels based on transaction volume over a 12-month period. Exhibit 1.7 summarizes the merchant level definitions based on annual transaction volume for Visa, MasterCard, and American Express. However, if a merchant has been the victim of a hack that resulted in an account data compromise, the merchant may be escalated to a higher level. Note, the JCB and Discover card brands do not classify merchants based on annual transaction volume. Refer to the Resources section for the Web site addresses for these payment card brands.

Level	Visa	MasterCard	American Express
Level 1	≥6,000,000	≥6,000,000 Also, merchants that experienced an account compromise	≥2,500,000 Also, merchants that experienced an account compromise
Level 2	1,000,000– 5,999,999	1,000,000– 5,999,999	50,000–2,499,999
Level 3	20,000– 999,999	20,000–999,999	<50,000
Level 4	<20,000	<20,000	N/A

EXHIBIT 1.7   Merchant Level Definitions Based on Annual Transactions

Based on their level, merchants are required to submit validation of compliance with PCI Data Security Standards. For MasterCard, Visa, and American Express, merchants must submit the following:

Level 1

- Annual on-site PCI Data Security Assessment performed by a Qualified Security Assessor *or* an Internal Audit if signed by an officer of the company.
- Quarterly Network Scan

Level 2

- Annual PCI Self-Assessment Questionnaire (American Express—not required)
- Quarterly Network Scan

Level 3

- Annual PCI Self-Assessment Questionnaire (American Express—not required)
- Quarterly Network Scan (American Express—not mandatory to submit except at the request of American Express)

Level 4 (Visa and MasterCard only)

- Annual PCI Self-Assessment Questionnaire (not mandatory to submit except at the request of Visa or MasterCard)
- Quarterly Network Scan (not mandatory to submit except at the request of Visa or MasterCard)

As you can see from the list above, all merchants are required to complete a Quarterly Network Scan. This scan, which must be completed by an Approved Scanning Vendor, is an automated tool that checks systems for vulnerabilities. It conducts a nonintrusive scan to remotely review networks and Web applications based in the externally facing Internet Protocol (IP) address provided by the merchant.

Like merchants, payment card brands also define levels for service providers. Exhibit 1.8 summarizes these level definitions for Visa and

Level	Visa	MasterCard
Level 1	All VisaNet processors (member and nonmember) All payment gateways	All TPPs All DSEs that store, transmit, or process more than one million annual transactions
Level 2	All providers that store, transmit, or process more than one million annual transactions	All DSEs that store, transmit, or process less than one million annual transactions
Level 3	All providers that store, transmit, or process less than one million annual transactions	N/A

EXHIBIT 1.8   Service-Provider Level Definitions

MasterCard. Note, American Express, JCB, and Discover card brands do not classify merchants based on annual transaction volume. Refer to the Resources section for the Web site addresses for these payment card brands.

CHAPTER 2

Security 101

A s discussed in the preface of this text, the Payment Card Industry Data Security Standard (PCI DSS) is built on a series of information security best practices that are widely accepted across many industries and organizations. An individual with a comprehensive understanding of information security best practices who is part of an organization with a mature information security program would likely face a manageable transition into PCI DSS compliance (since many of the requirements are based on best practices). For individuals not so placed, for those who must increase their knowledge of strong information security programs or implement PCI DSS into an organization with a new or evolving information security program, this primer will be invaluable.

Although information security is a complex subject and there are many intricate details involved in developing, implementing, and managing an information security program, it is critical to have a broad understanding of the requirements of a strong information security program. The technical ins and outs are not covered by this text, but we will examine selected fundamentals of information security as they relate to PCI DSS.

This discussion will provide a solid foundation for those less familiar with information security, as well as a review for individuals with a deeper understanding of the field. The information included in this chapter will help organizations trying to strengthen their information security programs and/or become compliant with PCI DSS requirements.

It would be a difficult, if not impossible, undertaking for organizations to become PCI DSS compliant without a rudimentary understanding of information security. The following information provides a broad outline of the information that organizations can use to develop, implement, and maintain a strong information security program. Depending on the level of maturity of an organization's program, it may not be essential to review all of these components. However, it is recommended to perform at least a cursory review, as many belong to the underlying principles required for a strong information security program and PCI DSS compliance.

STRATEGY AND PLANNING

Since it is impossible for an organization to achieve perfect security, the strategy and planning elements of an information security program are essential. Organizations have a finite number of resources and it is essential that a good plan be developed to ensure the maximization of these resources, effective security program implementation and management, and proper alignment with high-level organizational objectives. Remember that effective compliance strategies are developed to protect an organization's assets, not hinder its business operations.

Organizations can utilize a number of strategies, frameworks, methodologies, and approaches when developing, implementing, and managing an information security program, but there are certain foundational planning elements that should be included in the strategy and planning process. Exhibit 2.1 highlights these foundational elements and provides supporting examples.

INFORMATION RISK MANAGEMENT

Since all environments are subject to risk, organizations must implement a proactive process to address this risk. As with most enterprise initiatives, it is important to clearly define objectives and develop procedures to accomplish the organization's information risk management goals.

Planning Element	Example
Governance Model	• Centralized vs. Decentralized
Policy and Guidance	• External factors • Internal factors • Align with organization's goals and objectives
Capital Planning	• Risk-driven cost-benefit analysis • Outsourcing
Infrastructure/Architecture	• Selection that aligns with business strategy • Build vs. Buy • Legacy system issues
Operations	• Staffing • Operational resource requirements
Oversight	• Senior management support • Continuous program monitoring and validation/remediation of findings
Program Disposition	• Timely and appropriate disposition that aligns with business strategy

EXHIBIT 2.1 Elements of Information Security—Program Strategy and Planning

Information risk management can be defined as the process of identifying, controlling, and mitigating information system–related risks. It typically includes a formal risk assessment; cost-benefit analysis; and the selection, testing, evaluation, and implementation of appropriate safeguards. This process must be supported by senior management and include representatives from all of the teams impacted by the risk management processes. Organizations must consider the impact the risk management plan will have on the organization, as well as internal and external influences such as policy, business goals, and legal and regulatory requirements.

Now that we have a working definition of information risk management it is important to note a few critical points from our definition factors that impact a successful information risk management process. First, information risk management is a process. This means that it is continually evolving, adapting, and changing due to the numerous external and internal factors that impact an organization's risk environment and information risk management process.

The other key point to take away from our definition is the concept of cost-benefit analysis. Unfortunately, any component of the information risk management process that is not guided by this principle will ultimately prove to be unsuccessful. Any information risk management methodology that is too costly, too difficult to manage or a general hindrance to the organization will never add value and most likely will be abandoned by its organization. Remember, the point of information risk management is to help the organization achieve its business objectives, in this case by managing the risk associated with its information systems.

This perspective does not advocate ignoring appropriate protective measures just because they pose initial costs. Organizations must balance

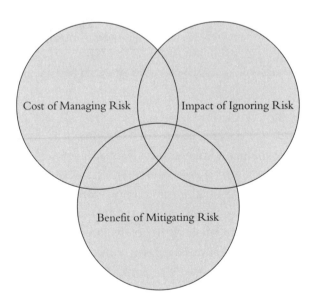

EXHIBIT 2.2   Risk Management Cost-Benefit Relationship

said costs against the benefits of security protections, always doing so in a way that promotes business objectives instead of thwarting them. Information risk management strategies and tactics must enable the business to operate in a secure environment but never prevent the organization from achieving its core competencies.

There are a variety of factors that influence the cost-benefit components of information risk management. Broadly, these break down into the cost of managing the risk, the impact of ignoring the risk, and the benefit of mitigating or eliminating the risk. Exhibit 2.2 represents the cohesive relationship among these factors. Organizations must remember that there will be a series of trade-offs in the cost-benefit aspect of risk management. The goal is to strike the appropriate level of balance between risk and cost, not eliminate risk altogether.

INFORMATION CLASSIFICATION

One of the most critical steps to implementing an information security program is the classification of the organization's information and associated systems. Unfortunately, many organizations overlook this important step and become focused on the technology requirements and operational details associated with an information security program. Although technology and operations are actually an important part of the process, they must be addressed after the organization's systems and information have been properly classified. Why spend your organization's valuable resources (time and money) safeguarding information that may not need to be protected?

Information classification has a broad scope and encompasses more than just data. In fact, it is best to view information classification from a holistic perspective. At a minimum it should include data, systems, user and system documentation, and operational and support documentation. Only after a comprehensive information classification schema has been developed can an organization transition to the implementation of tactical and operational safeguards. After the information has been appropriately classified, specific handling requirements and procedures need to be developed for each classification category. Furthermore,

Military/ Government	Example	Private Sector	Example
Top Secret	Military Defense Information	Confidential	Trade Secrets/ Intellectual Property
Secret	Military Logistics Information	Private	Employee Information
Confidential	Military Personnel Information	Sensitive	Financial Information
Unclassified	Military Recruiting Information	Public	Marketing Literature

EXHIBIT 2.3   Sample Information Classification Profiles

security controls must be implemented to ensure the intent of the information classification safeguards is adequately met.

There are a number of different ways in which organizations can implement data classification. However, most involve some type of a hierarchical structure with defining criteria that allow data to be categorized and prioritized. Most data classifications are based on either the private sector or military classification model (or a variation of one of the models). Exhibit 2.3 summarizes two models and offers a brief description and supporting example.

RISK ASSESSMENT

Before we can begin a discussion about risk assessment, one thing needs to be made clear. Oftentimes, the terms "threat" and "vulnerability" are used interchangeably. However, there is an important distinction between the two. A vulnerability can be defined as a deficiency within an environment that can be exploited by a threat. A threat is a potential danger that can negatively affect an environment. For example, if a building does not have a security system, the building is more susceptible to a burglary. In this example, the threat is being burglarized because of the vulnerability of not having a security system. This is not to say that having a security system will guarantee that the building is never burglarized. But the security system would serve as a safeguard that reduced the risk of the threat of burglary.

Risk assessment is the cornerstone of an organization's information security and risk management strategy. Only after investing the appropriate amount of time and resources in developing a risk assessment strategy can the organization move forward to an operational risk management plan. It is important to understand that there is no such thing as 100 percent security. Even if this were achievable, the associated costs would most likely be prohibitive and would negatively impact the financial well-being of the business. The risk management challenge lies in balancing appropriate levels of data protection against successful business operations. This balance can be achieved only after a thorough risk assessment of the organization's information assets and operating environment.

Before delving into risk assessment strategies, it is important to review one of the principal information security concepts. Confidentiality, integrity, and availability are the three primary drivers of information security. This information security foundation is commonly referred to as the *CIA Triangle*. (See Exhibit 2.4.)

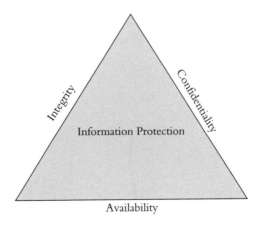

EXHIBIT 2.4   CIA Triangle

The CIA Triangle is a reference model that emphasizes the three components of information assurance. *Confidentiality* can be defined as the prevention of unauthorized disclosure of sensitive information. *Integrity* is a broader-reaching concept, intended to protect the information against modification by unauthorized users, prevention of unauthorized or accidental modification of information by authorized users, and the preservation of information. Since information is used in decision-making processes, it must be properly preserved in order to ensure that any action or inaction based on the information was made appropriately. The third leg of the triangle, availability, enables authorized users to have continual and reliable access to the information within the organization's environment. Now that we have a clear understanding of the CIA Triangle, we can utilize this methodology as part of our risk assessment process.

One of the more common methodologies used in the risk assessment process is to classify the data and associated information systems based on a CIA rating. This allows the organization to have an objective system for placing a value on the information residing in the network. Once this classification is established, a risk assessment can be performed. This risk assessment can identify the potential threats to the organization's environment.

RISK ANALYSIS

The best approach to risk management is team based, or at the very least the analysis process needs to be sensitive to all of the individuals and departments impacted by risk management within the organization. A collaboration of leaders and subject matter experts in technology, operations, legal/compliance, and finance are a great foundation for building an effective risk management team. Once the organization has selected the appropriate mix of people to perform the risk assessment, they are ready to begin the risk assessment process.

Risk analysis is the process of identifying the vulnerabilities, threats, and negative impacts facing the organization. This information is then utilized to implement appropriate safeguards and controls required to protect the organization. Regardless of the specific methodologies deployed by an organization to conduct risk analysis, the goals are:

- Determine the organization's assets and value of the assets.
- Determine the vulnerabilities and threats facing the organization.
- Determine the likelihood and impact of the threats and vulnerabilities.
- Determine the financial balance between the cost of the negative impact and the cost of the safeguard.

Risk analysis typically employs a combination of qualitative (use of judgment, best practices, and experience) and quantitative (use of real numbers assigned to costs, assets value, business impact, and threats and vulnerabilities) techniques to calculate the risk facing an organization.

A cost-benefit analysis will help an organization to make quantified and objective decisions regarding information security. Although from a PCI DSS compliance perspective it is a relatively easy decision (comply or face the consequences of noncompliance, as discussed earlier), the benefits of cost-benefit analysis can be leveraged in forming the compliance strategy, prioritization of compliance initiatives, and the selection of one compliance strategy, vendor, or tool over another.

If after a cost-benefit analysis an organization determines that the appropriate course of action is to mitigate a risk, it must find an appropriate safeguard. The definition of an appropriate safeguard will vary based on the risk being mitigated, since a company will not want the cost of the appropriate safeguard to exceed the cost of accepting the risk.

DEALING WITH RISK

Once organizations have properly identified risk, they need to develop a strategy to manage the risk. Remembering that there is no such thing as 100 percent security or a risk-free business environment, intelligent choices must be made. These choices must factor in the big picture. Organizations must strive to make decisions that balance the security of the cardholder data environment against the costs of reasonable protection mechanisms and safeguards. The organization will need to choose one of the risk management strategies listed below:

- **Mitigate the risk**. Implement a safeguard to reduce the impact of the risk and/or reduce the likeness of the risk occurring.
- **Transfer the risk**. Move or displace the risk to another environment (i.e., purchase insurance).
- **Avoid the risk**. Avoid the activity that presents the risk.
- **Accept the risk**. Choose not to mitigate, transfer, or avoid the risk because doing any of these would cost more than addressing the risk's impact.

DEFENSE IN DEPTH

The defense-in-depth security model is a layered approach to protecting an organization's information systems, data, and associated infrastructure. Conceptually this model relies on the idea that the sum of the organization's security protections is stronger than the individual security safeguards. In other words, since no one protection is strong enough to offer the organization a comprehensive level of protection, the individual components must work together to achieve the desired result. Additionally, this layered approach acts as a failsafe mechanism. For example, if one of the exterior components of the defense-in-depth approach fails, the entity is still protected by the existing internal layers of protection. Exhibit 2.5 represents a common approach to defense in depth. In this example, security protections are offered from an enterprise perspective. Adequate safeguards must be designed, implemented, and managed to address security from a holistic perspective (perimeter, network, host, application, and data layers).

POLICY, STANDARDS, AND PROCEDURES

As a best practice, organizations should maintain a policy that addresses information security for employees and contractors. There are some fundamental Security 101 concepts that should be addressed prior to

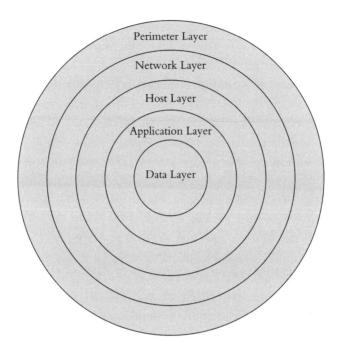

EXHIBIT 2.5 Defense in Depth

pursuing the numerous challenges and intricacies associated with an information security policy. Information Shield, a global vendor that offers information security policy tools and services, recommends the following seven elements for the development of an effective information security policy management program:

1. Written documents with version control
2. Defined policy document ownership
3. Defined management structure
4. Target user groups
5. An effective date range
6. A verified audit trail
7. A written exception process

Additionally, it is important to note the common terminology and frequent misconceptions associated with an information security policy.

Policies, standards, baselines, guidelines, and *procedures* are all different and each has its unique purpose, but they must be integrated together to strengthen and guide an information security program. It is best to think of a policy as a high-level strategic document that shows (from a senior management perspective) how information security is structured within the organization. A policy should be applied throughout the organization in a consistent manner and act as a reference for employees; they should be able to use it for guidance when conducting their everyday activities. Standards, baselines, guidelines, and procedures are the detailed operational protocols that support the policy, as shown in Exhibit 2.6.

Standards specifically reference the organization's mandatory activities, rules, and/or requirements. The standards are compulsory and usually refer to specific hardware and/or software. For example, an organization might specify a standard operating system or standard platform that must be used by all of its employees. By employing standards, an organization can implement security controls effectively across the entire enterprise.

A *baseline* can be defined as a point-in-time perspective that is used as a comparative reference point during a future change. Baselines

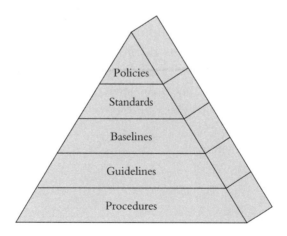

EXHIBIT 2.6   Policy Hierarchy

have a variety of purposes. One strategy is to leverage a baseline as a starting point that can be used to validate improvements within the organization's security program. Also a baseline can be an acceptable minimum level requirement for the organization.

Guidelines are the organization's recommendations when no specific standard applies. They are best utilized to address operational situations on a case-by-case basis, with action based on the specific circumstances. They should provide flexibility and allow users to implement security controls in more than one way. They also can be used to ensure that important security measures are not overlooked.

Procedures are the detailed step-by-step instructions that are utilized to achieve specific operational requirements. Procedures are detailed steps to be followed in order to accomplish specific tasks. Examples of procedures include the steps used in preparing new user accounts or assigning role-based access privileges.

ADOPTION OF A SECURITY FRAMEWORK

There are a number of security control frameworks that organizations can adopt to develop or strengthen their security posture. PCI DSS is actually built upon many of the best practices that make up the various security frameworks and methodologies. It is highly recommended that organizations select at least one of the common security frameworks listed in Exhibit 2.7. Some of the suggested frameworks are not specific to information security but can be modified to fit the organization's information security program requirements. Ideally, the organization will implement a best-in-breed approach. This means the organization would choose an assortment of safeguards from a variety of frameworks in order to employ a strategy most suited to the organization's specific needs.

Regardless of the framework selected, most security models rely on controls to achieve the desired level of security (based on the organization's risk assessment results). Controls are the specific safeguards that actually offer security protections. Controls are commonly divided into three types: management/administrative, operational/physical, and

Framework	Definition	Description	Sponsoring Organization
ISO Family (27001, 17799, 20000)	International Standard Organization's security management standards.	A framework of standards that provides best practices for information security management	International Standards Organization
ITIL	IT Infrastructure Library	ITIL is a cohesive best-practices framework drawn from the public and private sectors internationally. It describes the organization of IT resources to deliver business value, and documents processes, functions, and roles in IT Service Management!	Office of Government Commerce
COSO	Committee of Sponsoring Organizations of the Treadway Commission	Voluntary private-sector organization dedicated to improving the quality of financial reporting through business ethics, effective internal controls, and corporate governance	COSO
COBIT	Control Objectives for Information and related Technology	An IT governance framework and supporting toolset that allow managers to bridge the gap between control requirements, technical issues, and business risks	Information Systems Audit and Control Association (ISACA)

FISMA	Federal Information Security Management Act of 2002	FISMA imposes a mandatory set of processes that must follow a combination of Federal Information Processing standards (FIPS) documents, the special publications SP-800 series issued by NIST and other legislation pertinent to federal information systems	United States federal law enacted in 2002 as Title III of the E-Government Act of 2002
OCTAVE	Operationally Critical Threat, Asset, and Vulnerability Evaluation	A risk-based strategic assessment and planning technique for security	CERT (Carnegie Mellon University)
CMMI	Capability Maturity Model Integration	A process improvement approach that provides organizations with the essential elements of effective processes	Software Engineering Institute (Carnegie Mellon University)

EXHIBIT 2.7 Selected Information Security Frameworks

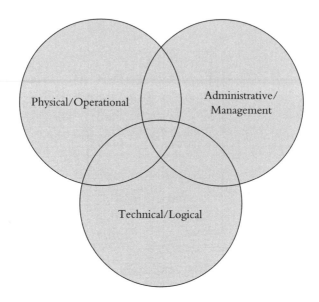

EXHIBIT 2.8   Security Controls Relationship

technical/logical. Although each category of these controls operates at a different level within the organization, the controls work together to provide a cohesive network of security protections. (See Exhibit 2.8).

Exhibit 2.9 summarizes each of the control type categories as well as offering an example.

Name of Security Control	Control Activity
Management/Administrative	Risk Management, Policies, Standards, Procedures, Training, and Accountability
Operational/Physical	Physical Security, Monitoring, and Incident Response
Technical/Logical	Logical Access Controls, Identification and Authorization, Encryption, and Audit Logging and Monitoring

EXHIBIT 2.9   Security Control Matrix

SECURITY AND THE SYSTEM DEVELOPMENT LIFE CYCLE (SDLC)

Today's organizations have a wide variety of technologies, strategies, methodologies, and tools available to design, build, implement and manage systems within the cardholder data environment. Regardless of the specific approach to systems development that an organization chooses, security plays a key role and must be infused into all phases of the development life cycle. When organizations proactively make security part of the early stages of the information system–development life cycle, they typically gain a significant increase in security for the cardholder data environment and with less cost than if they tried to achieve the same level of protection while implementing security after the SDLC.

Exhibit 2.10 shows the different phases within the SDLC. Although each phase includes a number of non–security related activities, those activities are outside the scope of this book. The discussion of each phase will focus only on the security-related activities associated with that phase of the life cycle.

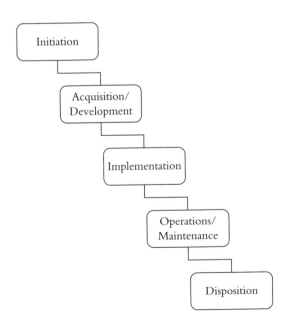

EXHIBIT 2.10   SDLC Phases

The first phase is the Initiation Phase. During this phase, the project participants should determine the security categorization of the system being implemented (high, medium, low) and determine the impact on the organization if the security of the system is compromised. Also, project participants should conduct a preliminary risk assessment that will provide a picture of the basic security needs of the system. Because of the nature of the Initiation Phase, the information needed to perform these activities may be vague or nonexistent, but performing these activities as best one can will help to select the proper security controls to be implemented along with the system requirements.

The second phase of the SDLC is the Acquisition/Development Phase. This phase should include eight security-related activities:

1. ***Risk Assessment***—This analysis should build on the preliminary risk assessment completed during the Initiation Phase. However, this assessment will be more specific and detailed, since the project participants will have actual specifications for the hardware and software that will be used to implement the system.

2. ***Functional Requirements Analysis***—Project participants should review the system's functional requirements to help determine the security requirements necessary for successful implementation.

3. ***Assurance Requirements Analysis***—Determine what development work and assurance evidence are necessary to establish confidence that the security will work correctly and effectively.

4. ***Cost Considerations and Reporting***—This will help determine how much of the project cost will be attributed to security over the life of the system.

5. ***Security Planning***—This activity will help to make certain that security controls are adequately documented. This plan should also include any attachments or references to other information security program documents (i.e., incident response plan, risk assessments, etc.) within the organization when appropriate.

6. ***Control Development***—Ensure that the security controls documented during the security planning activity are designed, developed, and implemented properly.

7. ***Developmental Security Test and Evaluation***—Ensure that any controls developed for the system are effective and working properly. Some of these controls, however, will not be testable until the Deployment Phase.

8. ***Other Planning Components***—Ensure that the incorporation of the security controls and requirements is in line with all the other components of the development and implementation processes.

The next phase of the SDLC is the Implementation Phase. In this phase, project participants will verify that the security controls meet the specified functionality. If they and all other functions of the system meet the specifications, the system will be accepted. Project participants will then need to ensure that the system is integrating correctly and certify that the controls are effectively implemented. During this process, the vulnerabilities of the system should be recorded. The final activity for this phase is security accreditation, during which authorization to access the new system is issued.

The penultimate phase in the SDLC is the Operations/Maintenance Phase. This phase involves continuous monitoring to ensure that the implemented security controls continue to be effective, especially as the system evolves and changes are implemented.

The final phase in the System Development Life Cycle is the Disposition Phase. Project participants will need to ensure that the information stored in the system is removed and securely stored and that the system itself is sanitized so that none of the data can ever be accessed via the system. Finally, the hardware and software should be disposed of as directed by the organization's information security policy.

SECURITY TRAINING AND AWARENESS

The organization's management team has the responsibility to ensure that employees are aware of their cardholder data protection responsibilities. Employees also need to know how to protect the organization's computers and networks from unauthorized use or compromise. When organizations create a security-conscious environment, employees become diligent in their daily routines and embrace their organization's cardholder data protection program.

Security awareness is the organization's overall strategy for educating employees on the proper protection of the cardholder data environment. Security awareness can have a significant impact on the protection of the cardholder data environment and reduction of unauthorized computer- and network-related activities. When organizations demonstrate that there are serious consequences for violating the security policy, they can ensure employees adhere to the security program. Employees who are found to be in violation of the security policy should be issued a warning, reprimanded, or in extreme cases terminated. When organizations follow these and similar approaches, management demonstrates the importance of complying with the organization's information security policy.

Security awareness can be reinforced through various communication channels. Some of the more common methods include posters, newsletters, general reminders in the form of logon banners and warning messages, or verbal communications presented at staff meetings. The greater the frequency and variety of communication, the more organizations will be able to increase awareness and protection of the cardholder data environment.

Security training is a more formalized and detailed process than awareness. It is an educational tool that is targeted to develop specific skills in the organization's employees. Awareness reminds people of their roles and responsibilities; training teaches people the skills required to fulfill their roles and responsibilities.

To ensure that information security training and awareness have been adequately embraced by an organization and have become a routine part of employee's daily activities, the organization must measure its level of awareness. The levels of employee security awareness should be reviewed at regular intervals to obtain assurance that awareness campaigns and training programs are effective. Questionnaires, assessments, and regular staff meetings can be used to measure employee awareness.

METRICS

The importance of information security metrics cannot be overstated. As Lord Kelvin stated, "If you cannot measure it, you cannot improve it." An effective metrics program enables organizations to objectively assess their progress against their desired goals. This information also offers a point-in-time snapshot of the organization's security posture. This information is essential for a variety of purposes. Some of the common uses by organizations include strategic planning, process improvement, resource allocation, and benchmarking. Exhibit 2.11 lists common metric frameworks that can be used by organizations when designing, implementing, and managing their metrics program.

Metric Framework	Description
Balanced Scorecard	A strategy-based performance management system that measures performance from the financial, customer, business-process, and learning-and-growth perspectives.
Common Vulnerability Scoring System (CVSS-SIG)	A vendor-agnostic, industry open standard designed to convey vulnerability severity and help determine urgency and priority of response. It solves the problem of multiple, incompatible scoring systems and is usable and understandable by anyone.
NIST 800-80 (DRAFT)	A strategic guide to developing information-security performance measures. Contains 17 control groups (access control, awareness and training, etc.) that align with NIST SP 800-53. (*Recommended Security Controls for Federal Information Systems.*)

EXHIBIT 2.11   Selected Security Metrics Frameworks

PHYSICAL SECURITY

Physical security is often viewed as the first layer of defense in a comprehensive information security program. Organizations will need to develop, implement, and continuously manage physical security programs with strong safeguards in order to adequately protect their cardholder data environments.

As with all foundation-level security controls, physical security draws its strength from a cohesive network of individual controls that work together to provide the appropriate level of protection for the cardholder data environment. Although each organization's cardholder data environment will require its own set of unique physical security controls, there are many commonalities that must exist in order for a comprehensive physical security framework to be put in place. Exhibit 2.12 displays relationships of the high-level requirements for a successful physical security program.

The ten requirements that every organization should consider when designing, implementing, and managing its physical security program are:

1. ***Physical Access Control of the Facility***—Preventive and detective controls that regulate physical access to the cardholder data environment

2. ***Inventory Controls for Media***—Control mechanisms that account for all media associated with the cardholder data environment

3. ***Monitoring Tools***—Tools and technologies that can monitor access to the cardholder data environment

4. ***Controls for Network Access Points***—Specific access controls for the physical protection of network access points (wireless access points, data centers, network infrastructure, etc.)

5. ***Visitor Identification Requirements***—Comprehensive controls that clear identify and manage visitor identification and activity

6. ***Security Storage of Backup Media***—Specific access controls for the physical protection of storage facilities containing backup media containing sensitive information from the cardholder environment.

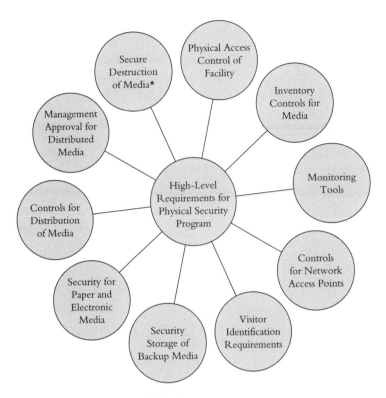

*Only media that contains cardholder data

EXHIBIT 2.12   Physical Security Program Requirements

7. ***Security for Paper and Electronic Media***—Specific access controls for the physical protection of storage facilities containing paper and electronic media containing sensitive information from the cardholder environment

8. ***Controls for Distribution of Media***—Controls that adequately regulate and protect the distribution of media containing sensitive information from the cardholder environment

9. **Management Approval for Distributed Media**—Well-defined process controls that ensure management approval for distribution of media, prior to actual distribution

10. ***Secure Destruction of Media***—Well-defined process controls that ensure secure destruction of media containing sensitive information from the cardholder environment

DATA COMMUNICATIONS AND NETWORKING

Although a comprehensive discussion of data communications and networking is outside the scope of this text, there are some fundamental concepts that must be understood in order to achieve compliance with the PCI DSS. Prior to addressing some of the specific data communications and networking technologies required to achieve PCI compliance, one needs to have a solid understanding of two common network models: the Open System Interconnection Model, commonly referred

OSI Layer	Description	Common Protocol Examples
Application Layer	The interface the end user uses to access the network	FTP, TFTP, SNMP, SMTP, Telnet, and HTTP
Presentation Layer	Formats data for presentation to the user	ASCII, TIFF, JPEG, MPEG, and MIDI
Sessions Layer	Initiates, maintains, and terminates logical sessions between end users	NFS, SQL, and RPC
Transport Layer	Establishes, maintains, and terminates logical connections between the original sender and the final destination of the message	TCP, UDP, SSL/TLS, and SPX
Network Layer	Determines the route a message should take through the network	IP, ICMP, RIP, IPX,
Data Link Layer	Manages the transmission from the Physical Layer and ensures it has no errors	ARP, RARP, PPP, and SLIP
Physical Layer	Transmits data bits over a communication circuit	X.21, HSSI, and EIA/ TIA 232 and 449

EXHIBIT 2.13   OSI Layer with Protocol Example

OSI Model	TCP/IP Model
Application Layer	Application Layer
Presentation layer	
Sessions Layer	
Transport Layer	Transport Layer
Network Layer	Network Layer
Data Link Layer	Data Link Layer
Physical Layer	Physical Layer

EXHIBIT 2.14   OSI and TCP/IP Model Comparison

to as the OSI Model, and the Transmission Control Protocol/Internet Protocol (TCP/IP) Model. The reason for this is that all network-related communications within the cardholder data environment are based upon the various communication protocols within each layer that make up either the OSI or the TCP/IP Models. The OSI and TCP/IP models are reference models that depict how communications on a network occur and provide a foundational level of understanding of network-based communications. In order to adequately protect the cardholder data environment, organizations must address the various types of vulnerabilities, attacks, and threats that could occur at each layer of the OSI or TCP/IP Model.

Exhibit 2.13 describes the components that make up the OSI Model. Exhibit 2.14 equates the levels of the OSI Model to those of the Internet Model.

PERIMETER SECURITY

Firewalls are the basic components of perimeter defense that organizations rely on in order to protect their internal network and the cardholder data environment. It is best to think of a firewall as a mechanism that restricts access from one network to another. Most commonly,

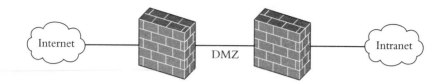

EXHIBIT 2.15   High-Level Firewall and DMZ Configuration in Broad Terms

organizations use firewalls to control access between the Internet and their internal network. However, firewalls can also be used to restrict access between internal network segments. For example, a firewall can be used to segment components of the cardholder data network from the remaining portions of the internal network. Authorized traffic will still have access to selected parts of the network, just not to the restricted areas containing cardholder data.

Another common use of a firewall is to create a demilitarized zone (DMZ). A DMZ is a network segment that resides between the protected and unprotected portions of the network. Oftentimes, the DMZ is insulated between two firewalls and typically contains Web, mail, and Domain Name System (DNS) servers. The external-facing firewall is used to restrict access from the Internet (or other publicly accessible networks). The internal-facing firewall is located in front of the internal network. The Internet is considered an untrusted network and the DMZ is considered trusted. The second firewall will control access from the DMZ to the internal network. Here the DMZ is considered the untrusted network, while the internal network is the trusted network.

In other words, the DMZ acts as a buffer between the Internet and the organization's internal network. An organization's specific infrastructure, the type of firewall it selects, and the firewall's configuration will vary. Exhibit 2.15 illustrates a DMZ configuration in broad terms:

INFORMATION SECURITY MONITORING AND LOG MANAGEMENT

Organizations that can successfully log and manage events within their infrastructure have an invaluable resource to protect their cardholder data environment. Depending on how it is implemented within an organization, logging and monitoring activity within the cardholder data environment can act as both a detective control and a source of investigative evidence critical to incident response and any subsequent legal proceedings. Despite these advantages, logging and monitoring can be a challenge. Furthermore, specific safeguards must be implemented to adequately protect the confidentiality, integrity, and availability of logs within the cardholder data environment. Each organization will need to address its own specific security concerns, but the National Institute of Standards and Technology's Special Publication 800-92, *Guide to Computer Security Log Management*, recommends the following minimum requirements for implementation of adequate log security:

- Limit access to log files. Users should not have any access to most log files unless some controlled level of access is necessary for creating log entries. If so, users should have append-only privileges and no read access, if possible. Users should not be able to rename, delete, or perform other file-level operations on log files.
- Avoid recording unneeded sensitive data. Some logs may record sensitive data, such as passwords, that does not need to be logged. When feasible, logging should be configured not to record information that is not required and that would present a substantial risk if accessed by unauthorized parties.
- Protect archived log files. This could include creating and securing message digests for the files, encrypting log files, and providing adequate physical protection for archival media.
- Secure the processes that generate the log entries. Unauthorized parties should not be able to manipulate log source processes, executable files, configuration files, or other components of the log sources that could impact logging.
- Configure each log source to behave appropriately when logging errors occur. For example, logging might be considered so important for a particular log source that the log source should be configured to suspend its functionality completely when logging fails.

- Implement secure mechanisms for transporting log data from the system to the centralized log management servers, if such protection is needed and not provided automatically by the log management infrastructure. Many transport protocols, such as File Transfer Protocol (FTP) and Hypertext Transfer Protocol (HTTP), do not provide protection. An administrator might need to upgrade a system's logging software to a version that has additional security features, or to encrypt the logging communications through a separate protocol such as Internet Protocol Security (IPsec) or Secure Sockets Layer/Transport Layer Security (SSL/TLS).

INTRUSION DETECTION AND INTRUSION PREVENTION TECHNOLOGY

According to the NIST Special Publication 800-94, *Guide to Intrusion Detection* and *Prevention Systems* intrusion detection is the process of monitoring the events occurring in a computer system or network and analyzing them for signs of possible incidents, which are violations or imminent threats of violation of computer security policies, acceptable use policies, or standard security practices. Incidents have many causes, such as malware (e.g., worms, spyware), attackers gaining unauthorized access to systems from the Internet, and authorized users of systems who misuse their privileges or attempt to gain additional privileges for which they are not authorized. Although many incidents are malicious in nature, many others are not; for example, a person might mistype the address of a computer and accidentally attempt to connect to a different system without authorization. An intrusion detection system (IDS) is software that automates the intrusion detection process. An intrusion prevention system (IPS) is software that has all the capabilities of an intrusion detection system and can also attempt to stop possible incidents.

There are a number of different intrusion detection and intrusion prevention (IDS/IPS) technologies, strategies, and architectures that can be deployed by an organization. The implementation should be customized to the organization's specific environment and business

Detection Type	Definition	Example	Notes
Signature-Based	The comparison of "signatures" against activity to identify possible incidents	Identification of known malware	Only effective for identifying previously known threats
Anomaly-Based	The comparison of identified activity to "normal" activity to determine any deviation	A significant spike in network traffic	Ability to identify new threats
Stateful Protocol Analysis	Comparison of protocol activity to "normal" activity to identify any deviation	Identification of a suspicious command	Resource-intensive detection methodology

EXHIBIT 2.16   IDS/IPS Detection Methodologies

requirements. Regardless of the differences among various IDS/IPS implementations strategies the following information must be understood before an IDS/IPS deployment.

Most IDS/IPS technologies use one or more of the detection technologies listed in Exhibit 2.16. Organizations must understand the differences so that they can select the appropriate detection methodology best suited for their environment and IDS/IPS needs.

Similar in nature to the number and variety of IDS/IPS detection methodologies there are also a number of IDS/IPS technologies. (See Exhibit 2.17.) Understanding the key differences will enable organization to select the appropriate technology to support the protection of their cardholder data environment.

Detection Technology	Definition
Network	Monitors network traffic for particular network segments or devices, and analyzes the network and application protocol activity to identify suspicious activity
Wireless	Monitors wireless network traffic and analyzes it to identify suspicious activity involving the wireless networking protocols themselves
Network Behavior Analysis	Examines network traffic to identify threats that generate unusual traffic flows, such as Distributed Denial of Service (DDoS) attacks, scanning, and certain forms of malware
Host Based	Monitors the characteristics of a single host or application and the events occurring within that host or application for suspicious activity

EXHIBIT 2.17   IDS/IPS Detection Technologies

LOGICAL ACCESS CONTROL

Logical access control and physical access control have very different practical applications, but from a broad perspective each kind of control follows a parallel intent. Both protection mechanisms are designed, implemented, and managed to restrict access to particular components of the cardholder data environment. The specific difference is that logical access controls occur within information systems and are part of a broader-reaching set of information security controls. This broader set of information security controls—identification, authentication, and authorization—are specific aspects that support the broader concept of logical access control. In other words, logical access controls function based on the successful operation of identification, authentication, and authorization control mechanisms.

As with the access control and authentication that occur in physical security, users must be properly identified and authenticated by logical security controls before being allowed into the cardholder data environment. This section will discuss the fundamentals of logical access control. The specific PCI DSS requirements concerning these concepts will be discussed later.

Logical access control is a broad subject with many components that work together to achieve the goal of restricting user access to the appropriate system resources based on predetermined specifications. Typically, this is done by applying the concept of Least Privileged Access Control, that of Role-Based Access Control, or a combination of the two.

Least Privileged Access Control gives a user access only to the information needed for effective performance of the user's job. Role-Based Access Control allows for differences in users' roles. For example, all staff-level accountants may have access to a portion of the information, but manager-level accountants will have access to that same information plus additional information appropriate to the managers' role. Of course, the information the accounting department gets access to will most likely be different from the information allowed to the marketing department. The benefit of implementing one or both of these concepts is that, if cardholder data is compromised or corrupted as a result of error or unauthorized access, the effects of the breach will be mitigated by the low number of people with access.

ELECTRONIC AUTHENTICATION

NIST Special Publication 800-63, *Electronic Authentication Guideline*, states, "Electronic authentication is the process of establishing confidence in user identities electronically presented to an information system." The publication goes on to offer extensive details and recommendations about electronic authentication that organizations can reference when developing their own organization-specific electronic authentication initiatives.

However, there are some universally applicable electronic authentication concepts to be noted. Authentication relies on factors to achieve its mission of validating that a user attempting to access a system is who they claim to be. The factors are based on the following:

- Something you know (i.e., a password)
- Something you have (i.e., a token)
- Something you are (i.e., a fingerprint or other biometric)

The term *single-factor authentication* is used to describe the deployment of one of these types of authentication mechanisms. *Multi-factor authentication* is the combination of two or more of these authentication mechanisms. The more factors that are used, the stronger the authentication process.

ENCRYPTION

When administered properly, encryption can be a powerful tool for supporting the overall security of the cardholder data environment. Effective information security management programs utilize encryption in a variety of ways to strengthen their overall security posture. The exact implementation of encryption technologies will vary from organization to organization, depending on intended purpose. But typically the technologies are used to protect cardholder data that is either in storage or transit. Encryption is used to alter plaintext into an unreadable format known as *ciphertext*. The encryption process relies on a special algorithm. The overall complexity of the algorithm determines the strength of encryption—in general, the more complex the algorithm, the harder it will be for an unauthorized user to decrypt the information. Most encryption algorithms are highly complex formulas that encrypt and decrypt between plaintext and ciphertext by using a special sequence of information referred to as a *key*. Since many encryption algorithms are widely known and used, the key is integral to the overall strength of the encryption.

Encryption methods fall into one of two broad categories: symmetric and asymmetric. Symmetric encryption methods use the same key for encryption and decryption. To maintain the integrity of the encryption algorithm, it is extremely important that senders and receivers keep the key secret; hence the term *secret keys*. Asymmetric encryption methods use two keys, one private and one public, with the public key being used to encrypt the information, the private key to decrypt it.

Since the security of an encryption algorithm is only as good as the security of its corresponding key, effective key management is critical to the security of the information being protected. *Key management* includes the ability to securely create, store, distribute, and properly

Encryption Method	Type
SHA-1	Hash
SHA-224	Hash
SHA-256	Hash
SHA-384	Hash
SHA-512	Hash
MD-2	Hash
MD-4	Hash
MD-5	Hash
AES	Symmetric
TDEA	Symmetric
TDES	Symmetric
RC4	Symmetric
ElGamal	Asymmetric
Diffie-Hellman	Asymmetric
RSA	Asymmetric
ECC	Asymmetric

EXHIBIT 2.18   Common Encryption Methods

dispose of encryption keys. All keys need to be protected against modification, and secret and private keys must be protected against unauthorized use and disclosure. Another category commonly associated with encryption methods is *hash algorithm*. A hash algorithm, unlike symmetric or asymmetric encryption, does not require the use of keys and is used mostly to validate the source of some given information. A hash algorithm will convert a longer string of information into a fixed-length string analogous to a digital fingerprint. In other words, this hash value is a unique identifier of an electronic source. Exhibit 2.18 lists some common encryption methods.

Exhibit 2.19 identifies how encryption can be utilized to increase an organization's overall security posture. However, it is important to note

Security Practice	Explanation
Confidentiality	*Confidentiality* is supported when encryption is used to translate plaintext to ciphertext that can be deciphered only by a key assigned to individuals authorized to access the information.
Data Integrity	*Data Integrity* is supported when specialized encryption algorithms (digital signatures, message authentication codes, hash, etc.) are used to identify any modifications to the original source.
Authentication	*Authentication* is supported when encryption algorithms are used to confirm the identity of the original information source.
Authorization	*Authorization* is supported when encryption algorithms are used to control access to a particular resource.
Nonrepudiation	*Nonrepudiation* is supported when encryption is used to validate the identity of an information's original source so that later the information cannot be disputed by the original source.

EXHIBIT 2.19   Security Practices Using Encryption

that one encryption algorithm can sometimes support a combination of the security practices in a single instance.

REMOTE ACCESS CONTROL

By a key component of its definition, Remote Access inherently has a number of security concerns. Although many of the fundamental concepts of access control (identification, authentication, and authorization) are still applicable to Remote Access Control, further discussion is warranted in order to address the additional security risk. Appropriate identification, authentication, and authorization are achieved by utilizing the following services to achieve a centrally administered remote access control program.

Remote Authentication Dial-In User Service (RADIUS) is an authentication protocol that is utilized in a client/server based architecture to authenticate and authorize remote users. The remote user accesses the network through a dedicated communications path (server, modem, DSL, ISDN, etc.). The user's login credentials are validated by the access server, and upon proper validation the user is granted access to the network.

SECURE COMMUNICATIONS

In order to adequately protect sensitive data during communications with the cardholder data environment, organizations must utilize secure communication methods. The following section highlights some of the more common methods that organizations can employ when communicating sensitive data. Each organization's cardholder data environment will have different requirements. However, all organizations must give careful consideration before selecting a particular secure communication method.

HTTPS

Before specifically discussing Hypertext Transfer Protocol Secure(HTTPS), we must understand its underlying technology, Hypertext Transfer Protocol. HTTP is a protocol residing on top of TCP/IP and is used for

Web-based communication between Web browsers and Web servers. From a security perspective, this protocol is a problem since the communication is unprotected and occurs in plaintext. In other words, anyone can intercept or interpret the communication as it travels from the Web browser to the Web server and back again. Hypertext Transfer Protocol Secure was developed to address this security risk. HTTP Secure can be summarized as HTTP running over SSL/TLS. (Remember that HTTP functions at the application layer of the OSI model and that SSL/TLS runs at the transport layer of the OSI model.)

SECURE SHELL

Secure Shell (SSH) offers a secure protocol that is used to log into another computer over a network. The tunneling mechanism enables a secure communications bath that can be used for secure remote terminal communications. SSH is a secure alternative to the less secure terminal service protocols (Telnet, FTP, rlogin, rexec, and rsh).

VIRTUAL PRIVATE NETWORKS

A Virtual Private Network (VPN) provides organizations with the ability to have secure remote access to the organization's internal network and resources. A VPN is a virtual network that resides upon a physical network. The virtual network provides a secure communications channel for data and other information to be transmitted between two communication devices or endpoints. Organizations can use VPN over existing public networks, such as the Internet, to enable the secure transfer of data. There are two main purposes to VPN access:

1. **Remote access**. Allows a remote end user to access the internal network via a public network (i.e., the Internet).
2. **Site to site**. Creates a secure bridge between two internal networks via a public network (i.e., the Internet).

Exhibit 2.20 lists some of the common VPN technologies.

VPN Technology	Description
IPsec	A protocol that provides security capabilities for IP-based communications (functions at the OSI network layer)
SSL/TLS/TLS Portal	Allows a user to use a single-standard SSL/TLS connection to a Web site to securely access multiple network services. The site accessed is typically called a portal because it is a single page that leads to many other resources. The remote user accesses the SSL/TLS VPN gateway using any modern Web browser, identifies himself or herself to the gateway using an authentication method supported by the gateway, and is then presented with a Web page that acts as the portal to the other services.
SSL/TLS/TLS Tunnel	Allows a user to use a typical Web browser to securely access multiple network services through a tunnel that is running under SSL/TLS. SSL/TLS tunnel VPNs require that the Web browser be able to handle active content. Examples of active content include Java, JavaScript, Active X, and Flash applications or plug-ins.

EXHIBIT 2.20   Common VPN Technologies

WIRELESS

Wireless is increasing in popularity and offers a wide range of benefits. Unfortunately, it is inherently more vulnerable to security threats. Although PCI DSS allows for wireless to be utilized (under specific secure operating configurations), we recommend that it be used cautiously. Specific wireless architectures, best practices, and security controls are outside the scope of this text, but it is recommended that organizations review NIST Special Publication 800-97, *Establishing*

Wireless Robust Security Networks: A Guide to IEEE 802.11i. In some regards, wireless technologies need to be treated in the same fashion as wired networks. In particular, all of the security concepts and best practices associated with wired technologies also apply to the wireless technologies. However, additional security precautions must be taken to adequately address the increased security risks inherent in wireless.

According to NIST, wireless networking enables devices with wireless capabilities to use computing resources without being physically connected to a network. The devices simply need to be within a certain distance of the wireless network infrastructure. A wireless local–area network (WLAN) is a group of wireless networking nodes within a limited geographic area that is capable of radio communications. WLANs are typically used by devices within a fairly limited range, such as an office building or building campus, and are usually implemented as extensions to existing wired local area networks to provide enhanced user mobility.

Organizations have come to rely on wireless communications because they offer organizations the benefits of portability, flexibility, increased productivity, and lower installation costs. However, organizations face increased information security–related risks when they implement wireless technologies into their environment. This increased level of risk occurs because there are underlying security risks inherent to wireless technology. Specifically, one of the most significant risks that organizations face when deploying wireless in their cardholder data environment is that wireless networks rely on communication through open airwaves. They are vulnerable to any and all threats that exist in the open air, and therefore they put sensitive cardholder data at risk. Furthermore, organizations that do not properly secure wireless infrastructure that is connected to the cardholder data environment face exposure to malicious attacks. Specifically, attacks can exploit weaknesses in the organization's wireless infrastructure as a backdoor into the cardholder data environment.

The following is a list from NIST Special Publication 800-48 Revision 1 (draft), *Wireless Network Security for IEEE 802.11a/b/g and Bluetooth*, of the broad risks facing wireless networks:

- Malicious entities may gain unauthorized access to an organization's computer network through unsecured wireless connections.
- Sensitive information that is transmitted without having been encrypted, or after having been encrypted with weak techniques, is vulnerable to attack.
- Malicious entities may steal the identity of legitimate users and masquerade as them on internal or external corporate networks.
- Malicious entities may deploy unauthorized equipment (e.g., client devices and access points) to surreptitiously gain access to sensitive information.
- Malware may corrupt data on a wireless device and subsequently be introduced to a wired network connection.
- Malicious entities may, through wireless connections, connect to other organizations in order to launch attacks and/or conceal their activities.
- Interlopers, from inside or out, may be able to gain connectivity to network management controls and thereby disable or disrupt operations.
- Malicious entities may use rogue wireless networks deployed within an organization to gain access to the organization's network resources.
- Internal and client device–based attacks may be possible via ad hoc transmissions.

INCIDENT RESPONSE

Incident response is one of the final components of building a strong information security program. In a perfect world this phase would not be required, as all of the protections in place would prevent an incident from occurring. However, we learned in our Security 101 discussion that an organization's security is only as strong as its weakest link and that defense in depth, or the layered approach to information security and data protection, is the best approach to take. Following this premise, incident response becomes the final layer. It is what we do when all other strategies have been exhausted. According to the CERT®

(Computer Emergency Response Team) Information Center at Carnegie Mellon University's Software Engineering Institute, a general definition of *incident response* is the response to any real or suspected adverse event in relation to the security of computer systems or computer networks. Even though incident response definitions may vary from organization to organization, this description of incident response offers a working definition for purposes of this discussion. The CERT offers a wealth of detailed incident response information that organizations can tailor to their specific needs. Nevertheless, there are some important commonalties to note when developing your organization's incident response program. Specifically, CERT Information Center recommends creating a Computer Security Incident Response Team (CSIRT) using the following eight best practices:

1. Obtain management support and buy-in.
2. Determine the CSIRT strategic plan.
3. Gather relevant information.
4. Design the CSIRT vision.
5. Communicate the CSIRT vision and operational plan.
6. Begin CSIRT implementation.
7. Announce the operational CSIRT.
8. Evaluate CSIRT effectiveness.

FORENSICS

According to NIST Special Publication 800-86, *Guide to Integrating Forensic Techniques into Incident Response*, the term *forensic science* is generally defined as the application of science to the law. *Digital forensics*, also known as computer and network forensics, has varying definitions among organizations, academics, and practitioners. Regardless of the variations in definition, *computer forensics* is generally considered to be the application of science to the identification, collection, examination, and analysis of data while preserving the integrity of the information and maintaining a strict chain of custody for the data so that the information can be admitted into the legal system. Any information gathered in such a manner that does not meet this general definition will likely be considered inadmissible in any civil or criminal proceedings.

Since there are a number of broad definitions surrounding digital forensics, it is best for organizations to maintain a broad perspective when applying a definition. Furthermore, they should remember the intent of the definition when determining applicability to their specific cardholder data environment. This will allow organizations to comply with PCI DSS requirements by designing, implementing, and managing incident response and forensic capabilities in a manner that allows the organization to respond appropriately in the event of a breach of the cardholder data environment. Keeping all of this in mind, organizations have an ever-increasing amount of data from a number of sources within the cardholder data environment. For example, sensitive cardholder data can be stored or transferred by the organization's computer systems, networking infrastructure, networking devices, and various types of media connected to the cardholder data environment. Due to the variety of data sources and connection points within the cardholder data environment, forensic techniques can be employed so the organization has the ability to investigate crime and internal policy violations, computer security incidents, and operational/performance issues. Because of the number of applications that forensics has within the cardholder data environment, every organization needs to have the capability to perform digital forensics. Remember that the organization as a whole should have this capability and that forensic capability does not have to reside in-house. In other words, incident response and forensics can be outsourced. The important takeaway is that organizations have a plan and can respond appropriately as needed, regardless of whether the plan is carried out by using internal or external resources. Without a forensic incident response capability, organizations will not be able to determine what events have occurred within the cardholder data environment during a data security breach.

Even though the specific forensic programs that are designed, implemented, and managed will vary from organization to organization, (especially if an organization elects to have forensic capabilities conducted by an external service provider), careful consideration must be given to ensure that the fundamentals of forensics are incorporated into your organization's program. According to NIST, at a minimum organizations need to have specific procedural/operational details that address the following broad components:

- **Collection:** identifying, labeling, recording, and acquiring data from the possible sources of relevant data, while following procedures that preserve the integrity of the data
- **Examination:** forensically processing collected data using a combination of automated and manual methods, and assessing and extracting data of particular interest while preserving the integrity of the data.
- **Analysis:** analyzing the results of the examination, using legally justifiable methods and techniques, to derive useful information that addresses the questions that were the impetus for performing the collection and examination.
- **Reporting:** reporting the results of the analysis, which may include describing the actions used, explaining how tools and procedures were selected, determining what other actions need to be performed (e.g., forensic examination of additional data sources, securing identified vulnerabilities, improving existing security controls), and providing recommendations for improvement to policies, procedures, tools, and other aspects of the forensic process.

PART 2

PCI Breakdown (Control Objectives and Associated Standards)

The division of this part mirrors the Payment Card Industry Security Standards Council's categorization of their requirements into six major control objectives:

1. Build and maintain a secure network.
2. Protect cardholder data.
3. Maintain a vulnerability management program.
4. Implement strong access control measures.
5. Regularly monitor and test networks.
6. Maintain an information security policy.

Each standard is written in *italics* in order to differentiate it from the review that follows it.

CHAPTER 3

Build and Maintain a Secure Network

The ability for organizations to build and maintain a secure network is the cornerstone requirement for Payment Card Industry Data Security Standards (PCI DSS) compliance. A secure network is the focal point of protecting the cardholder data environment. The organization's network and associated infrastructure enable payment card transactions to be conducted. Even though the PCI DSS approach to data security offers a variety of layered security protections, an unsecured network prevents organizations from adequately protecting the cardholder data environment. This chapter will review the PCI DSS requirements for ensuring an organization maintains a secure network that properly protects cardholder data.

REQUIREMENT 1: INSTALL AND MAINTAIN A FIREWALL CONFIGURATION TO PROTECT CARDHOLDER DATA

Firewalls are computer devices that control computer traffic allowed into and out of a company's network, as well as traffic into more sensitive areas within a company's internal network. A firewall examines all network traffic and blocks those transmissions that do not meet the specified security criteria. All systems must be protected from unauthorized access from the Internet, whether entering the system as e-commerce, employees' Internet-based access through desktop browsers, or employees' e-mail access. Often, seemingly insignificant paths to and from the Internet can provide unprotected pathways into key systems. Firewalls are a key protection mechanism for any computer network.

The first step to achieving compliance with this PCI DSS requirement is that the organization's firewall configuration standards must support the following detailed configurations (1.1.1–1.1.9). These requirements work in conjunction to establish firewall configuration standards to achieve appropriate levels of data protection and PCI DSS compliance.

1.1 *Establish firewall configuration standards that include the following:*

1.1.1 *A formal process for approving and testing all external network connections and changes to the firewall configuration.*

The term *change control* can be defined as a formalized process for managing infrastructure, software, and other related changes within an information technology (IT) environment. Specifically, in the scope of PCI, change control is essential to firewall configuration. In Chapter 2 we discussed how firewalls are used to control information flow into and out of an organization and to prohibit unnecessary access to the organization's internal resources. A strong change control methodology is required to ensure that unapproved or inadvertent changes do not negatively impact the rest of the organization. Although there are numerous business needs that will require an organization to make changes to its firewall configurations, these changes must be made cautiously and with appropriate approval. The strength of a firewall is only as good as its configuration. In other words, improperly configured firewalls create significant risk to the organization's cardholder data environment.

1.1.2 *A current network diagram with all connections to cardholder data, including any wireless networks.*

A network diagram is an invaluable tool for visually representing your network and all of the connection points to the cardholder data environment. The key part of this requirement is keeping the diagram current. Unfortunately, many organizations fail to regularly update technical documentation. One solution to this common problem is to include updating relevant documentation as a step within an organization's change control process. This is a viable solution since the primary reason documentation falls out of date is that it is often overlooked when changes are made to the environment. If the updating of documentation is incorporated into the change management process, the updating is less likely to be forgotten.

Due to the sensitive nature of network diagrams, it is recommended that they be handled cautiously. The same security protections and controls provided to sensitive cardholder data should be applied to cardholder-environment system documentation. If strong safeguards are not applied to sensitive network diagrams, they can quickly fall prey to malicious intent. System documentation and network diagram information are the blueprints to your organization's cardholder data environment. If discovered by a malicious attacker, the documentation becomes an excellent tool for compromising your organization's cardholder data environment.

1.1.3 *Requirements for a firewall at each Internet connection and between any demilitarized zone (DMZ) and the internal network zone.*

As previously discussed, a firewall is a primary external-facing defense and is used to protect, monitor, and control traffic both inside and outside of an organization's internal network. Thus, a firewall is a requirement at each Internet connection as well as between any DMZ and the internal network zone.

1.1.4 Description of groups, roles, and responsibilities for logical management of network components.

In Chapter 2 we discussed the benefits of access control methodologies based on the concepts of least privileged and role based permissions. Given these benefits, it only makes sense that organizations formalize the strategies into operational policies and procedures. Properly done, documentation of this information clearly defines the organization's management of logical network components. Increased levels of accountability, and ultimately security, occur when roles and responsibilities are clearly defined.

The "need-to-know" concept supports access control by allowing access only to those who require the information to effectively perform their roles and responsibilities within the organization. Organizations achieve the highest level of access control when they can segregate access criteria based on roles, groups, location, time, and transaction type. Exhibit 3.1 summarizes how each of these factors can be utilized to support a need-to-know based access control methodology.

1.1.5 Documented list of services and ports necessary for business.

The intent of this list is to provide an accurate inventory of services and ports that are required to support the business. The underlying security strategy is that only ports and services required to support the business should be enabled or configured. Many technologies have services and ports "open" by default. These unnecessary ports and services can pose additional risks to the cardholder data environment.

1.1.6 Justification and documentation for any available protocols besides hypertext transfer protocol (HTTP), and secure sockets layer (SSL/TLS), secure shell (SSH), and virtual private network (VPN).

Criteria	Description	Example
Group Based	Assigning several users (with same access requirements) to a group with appropriate level of permissions	The accounts payable department can access only the business's information relevant to accounts payable activities.
Role Based	Assigning rights to users based on job function	Accounts payable staff and accounts payable manager can all access accounts payable–related information. However, the staff will be assigned access to less of that information than the manager.
Physical/Logical Based	Restricting access to system resources based on physical or logical location	Data files can only be accessed locally (rather than remotely) by users that interactively log on (after properly credentialed and authenticated) or restrictions based on network addresses.
Time Based	Assigning access control rights based on time	Payroll information can be accessed only Monday through Friday, during the hours of 8:00 AM and 4:00 PM
Transaction Based	Assigning access control restrictions on data that is allowed to be accessed only for specific functions	Only funds transfers below $10,000 can be processed without management approval.

EXHIBIT 3.1   Access Control Methodology

Currently, PCI DSS, HTTP, SSL/TLS, SSH, and VPN protocols are the acceptable industry standards for electronic payment card transactions. Any use of protocols outside of these requires careful consideration and appropriate documentation before implementation. The use of additional protocols requires a strong business justification. Any deviations from these standard practices should be well thought out, have a strong business justification, and managerial approval.

1.1.7 *Justification and documentation for any risky protocols allowed (for example, file transfer protocol (FTP)), which includes reason for use of protocol and security features implemented.*

PCI DSS requirement 1.1.7 closely aligns with requirement 1.1.6. It is intended to address the use of high-risk communications protocols. The PCI Council takes the approach that high-risk communication protocols should be used only when there is an appropriate and well-documented business justification (when the business benefit outweighs the business risk). Additionally, the standard requires that security features are implemented to address the risk associated with using a dangerous communication protocol. When organizations are considering the implementation of dangerous communication protocols, they must give careful consideration to the associated risks and be sure that the potential benefits truly outweigh any risk to the cardholder data environment, especially when there are so many new technology alternatives available that offer less risk.

1.1.8 *Quarterly review of firewall and router rule sets.*

Firewall configuration reviews play a critical role in ensuring the ongoing protection of the perimeter. As any firewall administrator knows, it is all too easy for a rule base to become unmanageable over time accumulate rules that are outdated or simply incorrect. Regular reviews help remedy this effect and allow administrators to conduct a periodic rule set "health check."

This requirement is a proactive control to ensure that firewall and router rule sets are reviewed on a regular basis. Quarterly review is a reasonable frequency that does not place unnecessary burdens on the business but does offer a frequent validation cycle of the entity's firewall and router rule sets. The review should be conducted with a critical eye and the end goal of validating the rule sets to ensure alignment with PCI compliance and business strategy. Although the specific review requirements will vary from organization to organization, the following broad components should be considered in most organizations:

- Does the firewall/router rule set correctly support and implement your organization's information security policy?
- Are the firewall/router rule changes supported, validated, and approved by your organization's official change management process?
- Is your organization's firewall/router configured to properly log activity in accordance with your information security policy?

In addition to considering the information listed above, your organization must ensure that your firewall rule base is not hindered by extraneous rule-set information (such as firewall rules that are redundant/overlapping, outdated, or otherwise unnecessary). Managing firewall rule sets can quickly become a problem for your organization if you are not doing so proactively and failing to deal appropriately dealing with the associated hindrances many organizations face. The particular risk is that extraneous rule-set information could result in unintended consequences often caused by misconfiguration or routine error.

Although there are a variety of strategies, methodologies, and tools available for organizations seeking to be PCI DSS complaint to assist in firewall rule-set management, the underlying message to organizations is to design, implement, and manage a solution that allows you to keep your rule base simple, limit it to a manageable size, ensure it supports your organization's information security policy and PCI compliance program, and perform regular reviews to avoid any potential configuration errors.

1.1.9 *Configuration standards for routers.*

As discussed in Chapter 2, standards specifically reference the organization's mandatory activities, rules, and/or requirements—in this case, to ensure consistent router configuration within the organization's network.

Having a standard router configuration ensures accuracy and consistency within the cardholder data environment. A misconfigured router or a router that is noncompliant with the organization's standards can lead to increased risk from known vulnerabilities within the cardholder data environment.

1.2 *Build a firewall configuration that denies all traffic from "untrusted" networks and hosts, except for protocols necessary for the cardholder data environment.*

All traffic from unknown networks or hosts should automatically be blocked. By approaching firewall configurations this way, the unnecessary or accidental permitting of "untrusted" traffic flows can be avoided. Only business-required and PCI DSS–approved traffic should be allowed to enter the cardholder data environment. Although PCI DSS allows the some common network protocols (HTTP, SSL/TLS, SSH, and VPN) all protocol traffic should be allowed only if needed.

PCI DSS requirement 1.3 requires a firewall configuration that prevents connections from publicly accessible servers and any system component storing cardholder data. This is used as a primary, exterior defense to prevent any person on a public network from accessing sensitive cardholder data. Additionally, requirement 1.3 specifically notes the inclusion of wireless networks. Organizations often fail to account for wireless network components as possible intrusion points by malicious attackers. Wireless technologies are inherently more vulnerable to malicious attacks due to some of the underlying architecture and technical limitations. Fortunately, there are many recent improvements, strategies, and tools that organizations can use to increase security of wireless technologies.

The following subsets of PCI DSS requirement 1.3 detail the specific requirements of building a firewall configured to restrict connections between publicly accessible servers and the organization's systems that store cardholder data.

1.3 *Build a firewall configuration that restricts connections between publicly accessible servers and any system component storing cardholder data, including any connections from wireless networks.*

This firewall configuration should include the following. As previously discussed, firewalls can be used to restrict access from one network to another and they can be implemented in a variety of ways. However, configurations should be based on an organization's specific requirements while still complying with PCI DSS. For the purposes of this discussion, we are focusing on the use of firewalls to restrict access to the organization's private, internal network (the cardholder data environment) from public, external networks (most commonly the Internet).

1.3.1 *Restricting inbound Internet traffic to Internet protocol (IP) addresses within the DMZ (ingress filters).*

PCI DSS requirement 1.3.1 ensures that Internet traffic may not enter the organization's private network. Remember from our discussion in Chapter 2 ("Security 101"), that the DMZ is intended to act as an intermediary gateway that regulates inbound and outbound traffic in order to protect the internal network.

1.3.2 *Not allowing internal addresses to pass from the Internet into the DMZ.*

The purpose of this requirement is to ensure that firewall rule sets are configured so that any address that has been identified as internal or private is blocked from accessing the DMZ via any public accessible server.

1.3.3 Implementing stateful inspection, also known as dynamic packet filtering (that is, only "established" connections are allowed into the network).

This PCI DSS requirement further supports building a strong firewall configuration that restricts connections between the publicly accessible Internet and the organization's internal network containing sensitive cardholder data. Specifically, this is accomplished by utilizing a firewall configuration that implements stateful inspection (also known as dynamic packet filtering), a packet inspection method where packets of data are filtered based not only on the actual data contained in the packet but also on the connection used to transfer those packets. Therefore, once a connection has been established, the firewall is able to accept data packets based on the state of the connection without the need for subsequent individual packet reinspection.

1.3.4 Placing the database in an internal network zone, segregated from the DMZ.

A database should never be directly accessible from the untrusted public networks. It should be located in the organization's highly protected internal network. Since, as we have established, the DMZ is a protective gateway that controls connections to the cardholder data environment, the benefits of a DMZ are substantially diminished if a database is located within the DMZ.

1.3.5 Restricting inbound and outbound traffic to that which is necessary for the cardholder data environment.

PCI DSS requirements 1.3.5 and 1.3.7 are very similar in nature and will be discussed together. Both require that only information that is necessary to support the cardholder data environment be allowed through the firewall in order to reduce the likelihood of malicious traffic. Another effective strategy that nicely aligns with this control is to block all other inbound and outbound traffic that is not specifically allowed (PCI DSS requirement 1.3.7).

1.3.6 *Securing and synchronizing router configuration files.*

For example, running configuration files (for normal functioning of the routers), and start-up configuration files (when machines are rebooted) should have the same secure configuration. This requirement is in place to ensure both the security and consistency of router configuration files. When start-up configuration files are properly synchronized with live or current state configuration settings, the cardholder data environment is less vulnerable to unintended consequences due to system configuration changes. A standard routine event such as an operational reboot should not override existing settings. Also, appropriate change control and change management procedures apply here as well.

1.3.7 *Denying all other inbound and outbound traffic not specifically allowed.*

See the discussion regarding PCI DSS requirement 1.3.5.

1.3.8 *Installing perimeter firewalls between any wireless networks and the cardholder data environment, and configuring these firewalls to deny any traffic from the wireless environment or from controlling any traffic (if such traffic is necessary for business purposes).*

Although we have addressed many of the security risks associated with wireless networks in Chapter 2, if organizations choose to implement wireless networks, appropriate protections must be in place in order for the business to perform payment card–related operations in a secure manner. Specifically, requirement 1.3.8 mandates that perimeter firewalls must be implemented between any wireless networks and the cardholder data environment. This is because wireless networks are inherently insecure and a firewall placed in between such a network and the cardholder data environment offers an additional layer of perimeter protection.

1.3.9 *Installing personal firewall software on any mobile and employee-owned computers with direct connectivity to the Internet (for example, laptops used by employees), which are used to access the organization's network.*

By definition, personal firewalls are designed to protect a single host machine. Conceptually, they function with the same intent as enterprise level firewalls but with some subtle differences. By default, most personal firewalls allow outbound traffic originating from the source host and inspect inbound traffic. Personal firewall technologies are usually configured on a risk-based threshold (i.e., high, medium, or low settings, where *low* allows a majority of traffic through and *high* blocks most traffic). It is important to note that, since a personal firewall is based on a local host, centralized management and administration can be more difficult. Furthermore, in order to maintain consistency and PCI DSS compliance, the personal firewall needs to be configured and aligned with the organization's information security policy and enterprise level firewall policy.

1.4 *Prohibit direct public access between external networks and any system component that stores cardholder data (for example, databases, logs, trace files).*

As the Internet is a public network, open to anyone, an organization must block any direct access through the Internet to system components that store cardholder data. The following requirements prohibit direct public access and must be adhered to in order to achieve PCI DSS compliance.

1.4.1 *Implement a DMZ to filter and screen all traffic and to prohibit direct routes for inbound and outbound Internet traffic.*

As discussed earlier in this chapter and in Chapter 2, a DMZ is a security-oriented architectural model that is deployed to act as a buffer to screen traffic and prohibit specific inbound and outbound traffic. This requirement is used to prevent direct communication routes for inbound and outbound Internet traffic.

1.4.2 *Restrict outbound traffic from payment card applications to IP addresses within the DMZ.*

PCI DSS requirement 1.4.2 mandates that communication traffic originating from internal payment card applications is restricted to IP addresses within the DMZ. This ensures that sensitive cardholder data is not transmitted and ultimately accessible to the public Internet.

1.5 *Implement IP masquerading to prevent internal addresses from being translated and revealed on the Internet. Use technologies that implement RFC 1918 address space, such as port address translation (PAT) or network address translation (NAT).*

Internet Protocol (IP) masquerading is utilized to prevent an organization's internal network addresses from being translated and revealed on the publicly accessible Internet. Network Address Translation (NAT) and Port Address Translation (PAT) are strategies that can be utilized to achieve PCI DSS requirement 1.5, the implementation of IP masquerading. Broadly, NAT and PAT prevent Internet-connected hosts from being able to determine the IP address being used by the organization. If this sensitive network information were to be revealed, the organization would be more exposed to a number of threats. NAT allows any number of IP addresses to be translated to a different range of IP address. Since NAT hides the actual IP address, it is utilized with the organization's private IP address. (As defined by the Internet Engineering Task Force [IETF] Request for Comments number 1918 [RFC 1918] private IP addresses are nonroutable and cannot be used on the Internet.)

Unlike NAT, PAT is able to translate a number of IP addresses to a single IP address. The translation requests occur at the port level. The translating firewall or router uses a NAT table and assigns a port number rather than an IP address.

REQUIREMENT 2: DO NOT USE VENDOR-SUPPLIED DEFAULTS FOR SYSTEM PASSWORDS AND OTHER SECURITY PARAMETERS

Hackers (external and internal to a company) often use vendor default passwords and other vendor default settings to compromise systems. These passwords and settings are well known in hacker communities and easily determined via public information.

2.1 *Always change vendor-supplied defaults **before** installing a system on the network (e.g., include passwords, simple network management protocol (SNMP) community strings, and elimination of unnecessary accounts).*

PCI DSS requirement 2.1 offers protection against the malicious exploitation of vendor-supplied defaults. With the goal of easier system implementations in mind, most vendors deploy their software packages with standard configurations including default settings and passwords. These default settings and passwords are commonly known and readily available to anyone and therefore are easily exploited by any individual seeking to compromise the cardholder data environment. When an organization deploys a system or technology, it must change any default settings and passwords. This is also the time when any unnecessary accounts should be deleted. Typically, this includes the deletion (or at least disablement, if the system is not capable of deletion) of vendor support/maintenance accounts, guest accounts, and default administrator and unnecessary service accounts. It is also recommended to rename (to something that is not easily identifiable) any remaining accounts as well.

Additional protection is gained if the default settings are changed *before* the system is connected to the network. Changing the default settings in a postproduction environment substantially increases the risk of attack. Either an attack will be attempted before the settings have been reconfigured, or the reconfiguration will be inadvertently forgotten after the system is installed on the network, thus opening the way for attack.

2.1.1 *For wireless environments, change wireless vendor defaults, including but not limited to, wired equivalent privacy (WEP) keys, default service set identifier (SSID), passwords, and SNMP community strings. Disable SSID broadcasts. Enable WiFi protected access (WPA and WPA2) technology for encryption and authentication when WPA-capable.*

As discussed in Chapter 2, wireless environments inherently offer increased risk to the cardholder data environment compared with their wired counterparts. In order to increase security for wireless environments, PCI DSS 2.1.1 requires vendor defaults to be changed. The same logic requiring the removal of vendor-supplied defaults under requirement 2.1 also applies here. However, this requirement emphasizes the vendor defaults for Wired Equivalent Privacy (WEP) keys, Server Set Identifiers (SSIDs), passwords, and Simple Network Management Protocol (SNMP) community strings because these technologies are highly susceptible to attack if the vendor defaults are not changed.

The requirement also stipulates that SSID broadcasts be disabled so that an organization's access points are not readily visible to anyone with a wireless internet connection. Even when a password is required to use a specific access point, hiding the access point is still important. If the access point is harder to find, it is harder to attack. Authorized users who need access to the SSID will be given the necessary information to gain said access, further enforcing applicable levels of access control. Again, even when the SSID broadcast is disabled it is important to also change the SSID to something other than the factory default or an easily determined name to keep unauthorized users from "guessing" the name.

Finally the requirement mandates the use for encryption and authentication of Wi-Fi Protected Access (WPA and WPA2) when possible, and not of WEP, since it has been determined that access points using WEP can be easily accessed by hackers with a number of readily available software programs.

2.2 *Develop configuration standards for all system components. Assure that these standards address all known security vulnerabilities and are consistent with industry-accepted system hardening standards as defined, for example, by SysAdmin Audit Network Security Network (SANS), National Institute of Standards Technology (NIST), and Center for Internet Security (CIS).*

The security posture of an organization is significantly strengthened when it actively uses standardized system component configurations that have been vetted by leading security organizations. Organizations that utilize standard security configurations enjoy the benefits of consistent system component configurations in their environment, ease of management, and reduced risk. (It is less likely a system component will be configured in an insecure manner when configured to the organization's approved security configuration.) It is recommended that organizations adopt a best-in-breed approach by implementing configuration standards from a variety of sources. This allows the organization to cherry pick the best configuration standards in the industry and those that offer the best protections for the organization's specific cardholder data environment. Additional information and recommendations are available in the Resources section.

2.2.1 *Implement only one primary function per server (for example, web servers, database servers, and DNS should be implemented on separate servers).*

Compliance with this standard offers a variety of benefits. Specifically, if multiple critical functions are shared on one server, it becomes more vulnerable to attack because a malicious user needs to exploit the vulnerability of only one service in order to gain access to all services. Also, should that server be compromised, you lose more than if those critical functions were spread out across multiple servers. Under this model, if one server is compromised the additional critical components are likely to remain intact. Remember the availability component of the CIA Triangle (from Chapter 2). Availability is also increased by allowing only one critical function per server. If one critical function is temporarily unavailable, the remaining critical functions are still available.

2.2.2 *Disable all unnecessary and insecure services and protocols (services and protocols not directly needed to perform the devices' specified function).*

Conceptually, we have addressed the intent of this security control in our discussion of building and maintaining a secure network. Specifically, only services and protocols required by the device should be enabled, and only to support that device's specific purpose. For example, if there is no reason anyone will be trying to remotely access a machine on a regular basis, the ability to do so should be disabled.

2.2.3 *Configure system security parameters to prevent misuse.*

Although seemingly straightforward, this control is inadvertently overlooked by many system administrators. One reason for this occurrence is that, by default, many technologies are configured "openly." In other words, these devices are not configured with security in mind and must be hardened to increase security. Any part of the system not configured with appropriate security parameters is open to malicious activity.

2.2.4 *Remove all unnecessary functionality, such as scripts, drivers, features, subsystems, file systems, and unnecessary web servers.*

This PCI DSS requirement mandates that all unnecessary functionality be removed. The intent of this standard is to reduce the likelihood that vulnerabilities (stemming from unnecessary functionality and services) are exploited by attackers. Many of the excess functionalities are vulnerable to exploitation and could be inappropriately used to gain access to the cardholder data environment. The smaller the list of attack targets, the harder it is for malicious attacks to occur. Although there are times when business requirements must utilize technologies that have increased functionality, this is a case where less is more. It is highly recommended that organizations develop and implement additional security-oriented controls to reduce the risk associated with utilizing technologies with increased functionalities.

2.3 *Encrypt all non-console administrative access. Use technologies such as SSH, VPN, or SSL/TLS/TLS (transport layer security) for web-based management and other non-console administrative access.*

In this PCI DSS requirement, all nonconsole administrative access must be encrypted. One of the reasons for this is that many of the default nonconsole tools and technologies available to system administrators are not secure. These tools and technologies often transmit IDs and passwords in clear text (note the importance of this as we are talking about administrative level IDs and passwords). By utilizing a more secure transmission method or encryption technology (i.e., SSH, VPN or SSL/TLS/ TLS) the invaluable and powerful administrator ID and password are protected during nonconsole administrative access.

2.4 *Hosting providers must protect each entity's hosted environment and data. These providers must meet specific requirements as detailed in Appendix A: "PCI DSS Applicability for Hosting Providers."*

Requirement 2.4 is applicable only to hosting providers. The PCI Security Standards Council offers the following definition in the PCI DSS Glossary:

"Hosting Provider: Offers various services to merchants and other service providers. Services range from simple to complex; from shared space on a server to a whole range of 'shopping cart' options; from payment applications to connections to payment gateways and processors; and for hosting dedicated to just one customer per server"

In summary, entities that meet the definition of hosting providers have PCI DSS–requirement obligations that are twofold. First, they must adhere to all the same requirements as other organizations that must operate under the PCI DSS requirements. Second, they must comply with additional requirements specific to the security concerns faced by hosting providers. Requirements A.1.1 through A.1.4 (from PCI DSS Appendix A) address the additional security requirements.

REQUIREMENT A.1: HOSTING PROVIDERS PROTECT CARDHOLDER DATA ENVIRONMENT

As referenced in Requirement 12.8, all service providers with access to cardholder data (including hosting providers) must adhere to the PCI DSS. In addition, Requirement 2.4 states that hosting providers must protect each entity's hosted environment and data. Therefore, hosting providers must give special consideration to the following:

A.1 *Protect each entity's (that is merchant, service provider, or other entity) hosted environment and data, as in A.1.1 through A.1.4.*
A.1.1 *Ensure that each entity only has access to own cardholder data environment.*

Since the business model of a hosting provider is to offer technology-based resources in a shared environment, additional controls must be implemented to ensure that separate and distinct businesses do not have access to cardholder data that is not their own. These types of controls prevent the commingling of customer data.

A.1.2 *Restrict each entity's access and privileges to own cardholder data environment only.*

In spirit, this requirement validates the preceding requirement by saying, not only that entities must be granted access solely to their cardholder data environment, but also that they must be explicitly denied access to any other cardholder data environment.

A.1.3 *Ensure logging and audit trails are enabled and unique to each entity's cardholder data environment and consistent with PCI DSS requirement 10.*

PCI DSS requirement 10 specifically addresses the importance of the ability to track and monitor all access to network resources and cardholder data. As stated earlier, hosting providers must have these monitoring capabilities in place at the appropriate level required by PCI DSS compliance and implemented in a segregated manner for each unique cardholder data environment.

A.1.4 *Enable processes to provide for timely forensic investigation in the event of a compromise to any hosted merchant or service provider.*

The final requirement for hosting providers is intended to complement the previous requirements. Specifically, A.1.4 requires that in the event of an incident, adequate records exist to properly perform a forensic investigation. Hosting providers must have processes in place to quickly and accurately provide their clients with critical system information, as required by a forensic investigation.

Note: Even though a hosting provider may meet these requirements, the compliance of the entity that uses the hosting provider is not necessarily guaranteed. Each entity must comply with the PCI DSS and validate compliance as applicable.

The importance of this note cannot be overemphasized. Even if a PCI DSS–compliant hosting provider is used, it does not guarantee PCI compliance for the client organization. An organization that does not validate its own compliance, and instead relies on the hosting entity's PCI DSS compliance, is likely to fall victim to a false sense of security.

CHAPTER 4

Protect Cardholder Data

This chapter discusses the Payment Card Industry Data Security Standards (PCI DSS) requirements regarding the protection of the actual cardholder data within the cardholder data environment. Other components of PCI DSS focus on strengthening the perimeter, controlling access, and reducing vulnerabilities to the cardholder data environment. Protection of the cardholder data itself focuses on using various encryption technologies to safeguard cardholder data in storage and transit. Specifically, this chapter addresses PCI DSS requirements for general use of encryption to protect cardholder data, effective encryption key management, keeping the Primary Account Number (PAN) masked, and secure data storage and transmission methods. Although compliance with other components of PCI DSS helps ensure that the organization has a secure network, perimeter defenses, and strong access controls— all of which effectively keep malicious users from making unauthorized access attempts on the cardholder environment—it is important for organizations to deploy safeguards that properly protect the cardholder data in the event of a breach or other unauthorized disclosure.

REQUIREMENT 3: PROTECT STORED CARDHOLDER DATA

Encryption is a critical component of cardholder data protection. If an intruder circumvents other network security controls and gains access to encrypted data, without the proper cryptographic keys, the

*data is unreadable and unusable to that person. Other effective
methods of protecting stored data should be considered as potential
risk mitigation opportunities. For example, methods for minimiz-
ing risk include not storing cardholder data unless absolutely necessary, truncating cardholder data if full PAN is not needed and not
sending PAN in unencrypted e-mails.*

3.1 *Keep cardholder data storage to a minimum. Develop a data
retention and disposal policy. Limit storage amount and retention time to that which is required for business, legal, and/or regulatory purposes, as documented in the data retention policy.*

The intent of this requirement is to reduce the risk that
cardholder data might be compromised. The sooner that cardholder data is removed from the environment, the less vulnerable it becomes to abuse. If it is not stored, it cannot be accessed
inappropriately. Every business situation will likely require a
unique data retention and disposal policy that aligns with organization-specific requirements. However, the universally applicable message is that less is more. The sooner that cardholder
data is removed from the environment, the better the position
the business will be in to protect cardholder data. Additionally,
having a clearly defined and well-communicated policy that
aligns with business, legal, and/or regulatory requirements is
essential to support cardholder data protection and storage.
You cannot hold people accountable when such requirements
are not well defined and properly communicated throughout
the organization.

3.2 *Do not store sensitive authentication data subsequent to authorization (even if encrypted). Sensitive authentication data
includes the data as cited in requirements 3.2.1 through 3.2.3.*

PCI DSS requirement 3.2 operates on the premise that sensitive authentication data must not be stored after being used
in the authorization process. The PCI Standards Council takes
this precaution a step further by emphasizing that the data cannot be stored even if the data is in an encrypted format.

3.2.1 *Do not store the full contents of any track from the magnetic stripe (that is on the back of a card, in a chip or elsewhere). This data is alternatively called full track, track, track 1, track 2, and magnetic stripe data.*

In the normal course of business, the following data elements from the magnetic stripe may need to be retained: the accountholder's name, PAN, expiration date, and service code. To minimize risk, store only those data elements needed for business. NEVER store the card verification code or value or PIN verification value data elements. Note: See "Glossary" for additional information.

Organizations must keep in mind the importance of track data. Any compromise of track data's security would have a significant and harmful impact upon the cardholder data environment. PCI DSS requirement 3.2.1 stipulates that the full contents of any track from the magnetic stripe must not be stored. However, the standard recognizes that during the normal course of business, some data elements of the magnetic stripe may need to be retained. This data includes:

- Account holder's name
- Primary account number
- Expiration date
- Service code

However, this is one of those times where organizations must strive for the "less is more" approach. In other words, to minimize the risk to track data, only data elements required to conduct business should be stored. Furthermore, it is important to note that the requirement mandates that the card verification code or value or PIN verification must never be stored under any circumstances.

3.2.2 *Do not store the card-validation code or value (three- or four-digit number printed on the front or back of a payment card) used to verify card-not-present transactions.*

Note: See "Glossary" for additional information.

The document *Payment Card Industry (PCI) Data Security Standard: Glossary, Abbreviations and Acronyms* defines the card validation code or value as the element on a card's magnetic stripe that uses a secure cryptographic process to protect data integrity on the stripe and that reveals any alteration or counterfeiting. During transactions when a card is not present (i.e., for Internet purchases), this value is used to verify the integrity of the transaction. Due to the critical nature of this information, PCI DSS requires that the information is not stored. The underlying strategy behind this security protection is based on the fact that if the information is not stored and is used only during the verification process, it cannot be accessed by malicious attackers.

Each payment card brand uses its own term for this validation code as follows:

- MasterCard: Card Validation Code (CVC). This is a three-digit code found in the signature area on the back of the payment card.
- VISA and Discover: Card Verification Value (CVV). This is a three-digit code found in the signature area on the back of the payment card.
- American Express: Card Security Code (CSC). This is a four-digit number printed on the right side of the front of the payment card, just above the embossed account number.
- JCB: Card Authentication Value (CAV). This is a three-digit code found in the signature area on the back of the payment card.

3.2.3 *Do not store the personal identification number (PIN) or the encrypted PIN block.*

PCI DSS requirement 3.2.3 achieves the same intent as PCI DSS requirement 3.2.1. Although this requirement is specific to the PIN or encrypted PIN block, as opposed to the protection of the card validation or code, the requirement is utilized to safeguard against the same risk (unauthorized access to sensitive card information) while offering the same level of protection to a critical component of cardholder data. The information security protections offered by this control also operate in the same manner. If the information is not stored, it cannot be accessed.

3.3 *Mask PAN when displayed (the first six and last four digits are the maximum number of digits to be displayed).*

Note: This requirement does not apply to employees and other parties with a specific need to see the full PAN; nor does the requirement supersede stricter requirements in place for displays of cardholder data (for example, for point of sale [POS] receipts).

3.4 *Render PAN, at minimum, unreadable anywhere it is stored (including data on portable digital media, backup media, in logs, and data received from or stored by wireless networks) by using any of the following approaches:*

- *Strong one-way hash functions (hashed indexes)*
- *Truncation*
- *Index tokens and pads (pads must be securely stored)*
- *Strong cryptography with associated key management processes and procedures.*

The MINIMUM account information that must be rendered unreadable is the PAN. If for some reason, a company is unable to encrypt cardholder data, refer to Appendix B: "Compensating Controls for Encryption of Stored Data."

(Note: For easier reading, the requirements defined in Appendix B are analyzed immediately later in this chapter)

3.4.1 *If disk encryption is used (rather than file- or column-level database encryption), logical access must be managed independently of native operating system access control mechanisms (for example, by not using local system or Active Directory accounts). Decryption keys must not be tied to user accounts.*

Chapter 2 ("Security 101") discusses the various uses of encryption and the many common implementations and deployments used to protect the cardholder data environment. PCI DSS requirement 3.4.1 focuses on the use of encryption on data at rest or in storage.

Before delving too deep into this requirement, organizations must understand some broad but critical differences regarding data storage encryption.

Fundamentally, data storage encryption can be broken down into three broad categories:

1. Full Disk Encryption. Also known as *whole disk encryption,* this approach encrypts the entire storage device, including the operating system.

2. File Level Encryption. This approach utilizes technology that encrypts only selected files or folders.

3. Column Level Encryption. This approach utilizes encryption to selectively encrypt columns in a database.

The Payment Card Industry Data Security Standards demonstrate the three major storage-level encryption strategies and some of the advantages and disadvantages that organizations should consider when selecting their data-storage encryption strategy. (see Exhibit 4.1).

As each organization's cardholder data environment will have unique requirements, one or more of the strategies will need to be adopted to meet PCI DSS data-storage encryption requirements. For example, some organizations may find it best to implement full disk encryption on their laptops and mobile devices, column-level encryption on their databases containing sensitive cardholder data, and file level encryption on systems that support payment card transactions.

This requirement addresses two data-protection concerns associated with encryption. First, if whole disk encryption is implemented, the PCI Security Standards Council requires that logical access control be managed independently of the native operating system. Second, the decryption keys must not be associated to the user accounts. This is an encryption best practice that reduces the risk of the encryption mechanism being compromised, since the value of encryption is quickly dissolved when a malicious user has the ability to use the encryption key to unlock the encrypted information. Compromised keys can be stolen, modified, or used by unauthorized users. A number of factors must be considered when organizations implement key management

Data-Storage Encryption Type	Advantages	Disadvantages
Full/Whole Disk Encryption	• Everything on the drive is encrypted • Encryption automatically occurs—not reliant on user • Transparent to user • Many projects can be configured to support pre-boot authentication (which offers an additional layer of security)	• Increased processing time/potential performance issues • If passwords are forgotten by the user, data may not be obtainable • Recovery of data may not be possible if there are encryption software failures or software corruption
File/Folder Level Encryption	• Increased selectivity/granularity of items to be encrypted • May be integrated with access control/file restriction mechanisms • If the file is removed from one storage device to another, no further action is required as the information is already encrypted • Limited impact on system resources and reduced performance issues • Some products can incorporate logging and auditing capabilities	• Relies on user to properly select which information needs to be encrypted • Potential performance issues with backup processes • Additional key management resources required
Database/Column Level Encryption	• Reduces performance issues of database since only selected columns are encrypted • Offers alignment with segregation of duty security controls (system administrators will not see sensitive data during administrative functions because it is encrypted)	• Requires strict alignment with database • Significant impact on database design (difficult to implement to production phase database) • Significant key management issues

EXHIBIT 4.1 Advantages and Disadvantages of Data Storage Strategies

programs. Controls must be developed in order to maintain the confidentiality, availability, and integrity of cryptographic keys required by PCI DSS. Specifically, secure key generation, assignment, distribution, transmission, use, storage, and destruction must be addressed by the PCI DSS–compliant organization.

PCI DSS APPENDIX B: COMPENSATING CONTROLS FOR REQUIREMENT 3.4

For companies unable to render cardholder data unreadable (e.g., by encryption) due to technical constraints or business limitations, compensating controls may be considered. Only companies that have undertaken a risk analysis and have legitimate technological or documented business constraints can consider the use of compensating controls to achieve compliance. Companies that consider compensating controls for rendering cardholder data unreadable must understand the risk to the data posed by maintaining readable cardholder data. Generally, the controls must provide additional protection to mitigate any additional risk posed by maintaining readable cardholder data. The controls considered must be in addition to controls required in the PCI DSS, and must satisfy the "Compensating Controls" definition in the PCI DSS Glossary. Compensating controls may consist of either a device or combination of devices, applications, and controls that meet all of the following conditions:

1. *Provide additional segmentation/abstraction (for example, at the network-layer)*
2. *Provide ability to restrict access to cardholder data or databases based on the following criteria:*
   - *IP address/Mac address*
   - *Application/service*
   - *User accounts/groups*
   - *Data type (packet filtering)*

3.   *Restrict logical access to the database*

    ▪ *Control logical access to the database independent of Active Directory or Lightweight Directory Access Protocol (LDAP)*

4.   *Prevent/detect common application or database attacks (for example, SQL injection).*

3.5 *Protect encryption keys used for encryption of cardholder data against both disclosure and misuse.*

    PCI DSS requirement 3.5 emphasizes the importance of protecting the encryption keys against disclosure and misuse. Remembering how encryption works, we see how critical the safety of encryption keys is to the overall protection of encrypted cardholder data. In other words, regardless of how strong the encryption algorithm is, a misused or improperly disclosed encryption key potentially voids any of the benefits encryption offers in the protection of the cardholder data environment.

3.5.1 *Restrict access to keys to the fewest number of custodians necessary.*

    PCI DSS requirement 3.5.1 continues with the premise that the strength of encryption lies in proper key management and key protection. When someone has the keys to an encryption algorithm, they have complete control over the information being protected. The fewer people who have access to encryption keys, the better. They must be authorized, and having key access must be vital to doing their jobs. Proper management of encryption keys is similar to the proper management of physical keys. The lock will offer protection only from those without keys. Anyone who holds the key can open the lock. This control really comes down to a numbers game. The fewer number of people with key access, the less likely the keys will be compromised. Additionally, if the keys are compromised, it is much easier to investigate a smaller number of people than a larger group when determining the depth of compromise.

3.5.2 *Store keys securely in the fewest possible locations and forms.*

This control is very similar to PCI DSS requirement 3.5.1. However, this time the control focuses on the location and form of key storage, not on people. Interestingly, many of the same issues still exist. The intent of the standard is to protect the key from being compromised (as anyone who holds the key can access the encrypted information). This protection comes down to reducing the likelihood of a compromise and offers better investigative insight in the event of one.

Compliance with PCI DSS requirement 3.6 is achieved when the organization documents and implements procedures to address the information security control requirements associated with key management as addressed by requirements 3.6.1 through 3.6.10. As key management can vary from organization to organization based on a variety of factors (e.g., infrastructure, cryptographic technologies deployed, purpose of cryptography, volume of users/transactions, etc.), specific recommendations are outside the scope of this discussion. However, the spirit of these requirements, as well as the overall recommendation, is to develop organization-specific practices and controls that address the common key-management issues summarized in PCI DSS requirements 3.6.1 through 3.6.10. Organizations seeking further details on key management can leverage the recommendations from the National Institute of Standards and Technology (NIST) or the Resources and References sections of this text.

3.6 *Fully document and implement all key management processes and procedures for keys used for encryption of cardholder data, including the following:*

3.6.1 *Generation of strong keys.*

Since the strength of encryption relies on the strength of its keys, strong keys must be generated to protect the cardholder data environment. As with weak passwords, encryption keys that have been inadequately generated can be easily compromised.

3.6.2 *Secure key distribution.*

Closely aligned with strong key generation is secure key distribution. If keys are poorly distributed, the organization increases the likelihood of the keys falling into the wrong hands, ultimately leading to compromised encryption keys. PCI DSS requirement 3.6.2 requires an organization to design, implement, and manage a comprehensive key distribution process. Although this process will vary among different organizations, based on each organization's specific operating requirements, the overall theme of secure distribution must be remembered.

3.6.3 *Secure key storage.*

PCI DSS requirement 3.6.3 mandates the secure storage of encryption keys. Although seemingly obvious, the importance of the concept cannot be overstated. Since much of encryption's strength is reliant on the integrity of the corresponding key, the key must be stored in a secure manner. The same criteria associated with secure storage of any valuable item also apply to secure encryption key storage. The storage area must be impenetrable, have strict access control, and have associated systems to document details (i.e., who, what, when, where, why, etc.) relevant to access of the secure storage area.

3.6.4 *Periodic changing of keys.*

- As deemed necessary and recommended by the associated application (for example, rekeying), preferably performed automatically
- At least annually

The exact deployment PCI DSS requirement 3.6.4 will likely vary among organizations, based on the specific encryption technology utilized by the organization to adequately protect the cardholder data environment.

However, the intent of the requirement is universally consistent: to increase the integrity of the keys by changing them on a periodic basis. This is similar in nature to the security best practice that recommends frequent changing of passwords. The integrity of the password or encryption key is significantly increased when changed on a periodic basis. This requirement goes on to mandate that, at a minimum, the periodic changing of encryption keys occur annually. Finally, the requirement indicates that, where possible, the changing of the encryption keys should occur automatically. When an organization has the ability to rely on automatic encryption key changes, the organization reduces the likelihood of human error and gains efficiency through automated processes.

3.6.5 *Destruction of old keys.*

PCI DSS requirement 3.6.5 mandates that old encryption keys are destroyed. The strategic safeguard driving this requirement is that when something as critical as an encryption key is no longer required, it should be destroyed to prevent unauthorized use. The destruction of old encryption keys significantly reduces the likelihood that the keys will fall prey/victim to unauthorized use. In other words, if an old encryption key is destroyed, it is not available for accidental, unauthorized, or malicious use.

3.6.6 *Split knowledge and establishment of dual control of keys (so that it requires two or three people, each knowing only their part of the key, to reconstruct the whole key).*

PCI DSS requirement 3.6.6 is based on a traditional security best practice of dual authorization and could be considered to be analogous to the concept of segregation of duties. In dual authorization–based controls, two or more parties are required to validate and/or approve an action before it is carried out. This ensures proper authorization and agreement among responsible parties that the action should be performed. A common example of the approach occurs with financial disbursements. Prior to final disbursement, a check will require two authorization signatures. This security control methodology is applied to the control of encryption keys. Specifically, organizations are required to split the knowledge and establish dual control of keys among two or more authorized individuals. It also requires that each party have specific knowledge only of its part of the encryption key, to avoid inappropriate or unauthorized key reconstruction.

3.6.7 *Prevention of unauthorized substitution of keys.*

PCI DSS requirement 3.6.7 mandates that the organization design, implement, and manage a comprehensive control mechanism that prevents the unauthorized substitution of keys. This requirement is intended to prevent unauthorized users from substituting encryption keys. If an unauthorized user has the ability to substitute an encryption key, the user can maliciously subvert the organization's encryption key safeguards and pose substantial risk to the cardholder data environment. This could occur because the encryption key is the foundation of encryption's strength: He who holds the key controls the encryption algorithm and ultimately the integrity of sensitive cardholder data.

3.6.8 *Replacement of known or suspected compromised keys.*

In order to be compliant with PCI DSS, organizations must replace known or suspected compromised encryption keys as soon as they learn of compromise. As previously stated, the strength of encryption relies on the security and integrity of the supporting/associated encryption key. If known or suspected compromised encryption keys are not replaced, the organization is at the mercy of the individual who has caused the compromise. Organizations that do not promptly respond to known or suspected encryption key compromise are not only out of compliance with PCI DSS requirement 3.6.8 but also place their cardholder data environment at substantial risk.

3.6.9 *Revocation of old or invalid keys.*

PCI DSS requirement 3.6.9 nicely complements PCI DSS requirement 3.6.8 and is intended to offer similar safeguards for an organization's cardholder data environment. Although there is a distinction between knowing and suspecting that an encryption key is compromised, old, or invalid, the standards are in place to address the same risk to the cardholder data environment. Encryption keys that are old or invalid should promptly be removed and otherwise made unavailable. This revocation of encryption keys significantly reduces the likelihood that the keys will be utilized in an unauthorized manner. In other words, if the keys are revoked and not available for accidental or intentional misuse, the encryption keys can directly cause harm to the cardholder data environment.

3.6.10 *Requirement for key custodians to sign a form stating that they understand and accept their key-custodian responsibilities.*

This particular control is an administrative control that derives its strength and security protection from the concept of individual accountability. This high degree of individual accountability offers significant protection to the cardholder data environment. When someone is asked to sign and accept full responsibility for their encryption key, their level of commitment to the protection of that key substantially increases. They have a vested interested in overall protection and integrity of the encryption key.

REQUIREMENT 4: ENCRYPT TRANSMISSION OF CARDHOLDER DATA ACROSS OPEN PUBLIC NETWORKS

Sensitive information must be encrypted during transmission over networks that are easy and common for a hacker to intercept, modify, and divert data while in transit.

4.1 *Use strong cryptography and security protocols such as secure sockets layer (SSL/TLS) / transport layer security (TLS) and Internet protocol security (IPSEC) to safeguard sensitive cardholder data* *during transmission over open, public networks. Examples of open, public networks that are in scope of the PCI DSS are the Internet, WiFi (IEEE 802.11x), global system for mobile communications (GSM), and general packet radio service (GPRS).*

4.1.1 *For wireless networks transmitting cardholder data, encrypt the transmissions by using WiFi protected access (WPA or WPA2) technology, IPSEC VPN, or SSL/TLS/TLS. Never rely exclusively on wired equivalent privacy (WEP) to protect confidentiality and access to a wireless LAN. If WEP is used, do the following:*

- *Use with a minimum 104-bit encryption key and 24 bit-initialization value*
- *Use ONLY in conjunction with WiFi protected access (WPA or WPA2) technology, VPN, or SSL/TLS/TLS*
- *Rotate shared WEP keys quarterly (or automatically if the technology permits)*
- *Rotate shared WEP keys whenever there are changes in personnel with access to keys*
- *Restrict access based on media access code (MAC) address.*

Unencrypted data that is transmitted across the open public networks is vulnerable to attack. SSL/TLS and IPSEC are secure protocols that can protect sensitive data during the transmission/transaction process. These secure protocols were specifically engineered to protect sensitive data transmissions over public networks. Fundamental information about SSL/TLS and IPSEC can be found in Chapter 2 of this book, and more detailed information can be found in the book's Resources section.

4.2 *Never send unencrypted PANs by e-mail.*

PCI DSS requirement 4.2 mandates that primary account numbers (PANs), must never be sent unencrypted by email. A majority of e-mail systems and traffic are not encrypted by default. This means that, unless specific actions are taken to either encrypt the communications channel or contents of an email, the information is transmitted in plaintext. Email communications transmitted under default configurations are vulnerable to exploitation by malicious users.

CHAPTER 5

Maintain a Vulnerability Management Program

S ince technology is an ever-changing phenomenon, it is inherently and highly susceptible to vulnerabilities. With the constant change and improvement associated with technology, new threats and vulnerabilities develop at the same pace. Organizations that do not maintain a comprehensive vulnerability management program are not only facing noncompliance with Payment Card Industry Data Security Standards (PCI DSS) but also place cardholder data at extreme and unnecessary risk. There are a number of tools, technologies, and techniques available to address vulnerabilities and ultimately offer increased protection of the cardholder data environment. In this chapter, we will discuss the specific PCI DSS requirements regarding the use of antivirus software and security patches in order to minimize the overall vulnerability of the cardholder data environment. Additionally, this chapter addresses the importance of following information security guidelines such as those set forth by the Open Web Application Security Project (OWASP).

REQUIREMENT 5: USE AND REGULARLY UPDATE ANTIVIRUS SOFTWARE

Many vulnerabilities and malicious viruses enter the network via employees' e-mail activities. Anti-virus software must be used on all systems commonly affected by viruses to protect systems from malicious software.

5.1 *Deploy anti-virus software on all systems commonly affected by viruses (particularly personal computers and servers).*

The term *malicious code or software* (also referred to as *malware)* describes any software designed specifically for the purpose of bypassing, harming, or infiltrating a computer or network, including viruses, spyware, and worms. Malicious code can enter an environment in many ways, including by email, files downloaded from the Internet, or, in the case of worms, by exploiting vulnerabilities within a network. Exhibit 5.1 describes some of the more common forms of malware.

Name	Description
Macro Viruses	When viruses are discovered in Microsoft applications, they are typically macro viruses. These viruses attach themselves to an application's initialization sequence and then replicate themselves and attache to other areas within the computer or network when the application is opened.
File Infectors	These virus types typically infect .com or .exe files. When the files are executed, the file infectors will replicate themselves and attach to other areas within the computer or network.
Worms	Unlike viruses, worms typically impair networks, as opposed to files or a specific computer, and do not need to attach themselves to a specific application in order to replicate.
Trojan Horses	Trojan horses differ from viruses in that they do not replicate. Typically, this type of malicious code is used to install a "backdoor program" that creates vulnerabilities within a system or network.
Stealth Viruses	These viruses will "trick" virus scanning software so that an infected file will appear to be clean.

EXHIBIT 5.1   Common Forms of Malware

With the ever-growing problem of malicious software (including viruses), properly deploying, managing, and maintaining antivirus software within the cardholder environment is essential. However, deploying antivirus solutions is not enough. The software needs to be continuously updated and maintained. As new malicious code threats are constantly surfacing, organizations must keep up with the software vendors' updates. The antivirus solution is only as good as the defense software's most current version.

5.1.1 *Ensure the antivirus programs are capable of detecting, removing, and protecting against other forms of malicious software, including spyware and adware.*

Essentially, the intent of this standard is identical with requirement 5.1. However, it specifically requires that the antivirus solution be capable of protecting the cardholder environment from other forms of malicious code, specifically spyware and adware. These are particularly called out because they are currently causing a lot of malicious code–related issues and threats to the cardholder data.

5.2 *Ensure that all antivirus mechanisms are current, actively running, and capable of generating audit logs.*

We have already discussed the importance of antivirus software being current. It is also important to note that the antivirus solution should be configured in such a manner that it cannot be disabled by the end user. The solution protects cardholder data only when it is current and actively running in the environment. Although we will discuss logging later in this book, this component of PCI DSS requires that the antivirus solution be capable of generating audit logs.

REQUIREMENT 6: DEVELOP AND MAINTAIN SECURE SYSTEMS AND APPLICATIONS

Unscrupulous individuals use security vulnerabilities to gain privileged access to systems. Many of these vulnerabilities are fixed by vendor-provided security patches. All systems must have the most recently released, appropriate software patches to protect against exploitation by employees, external hackers, and viruses. Note: Appropriate software patches are those patches that have been evaluated and tested sufficiently to determine that the patches do not conflict with existing security configurations. For in-house developed applications, numerous vulnerabilities can be avoided by using standard system development processes and secure coding techniques.

6.1 *Ensure that all system components and software have the latest vendor-supplied security patches installed. Install relevant security patches within one month of release.*

The control that supports PCI DSS requirement 6.1 is similar to antivirus, firewall, and configuration standards security defenses in that they are only effective when current and properly managed. New vulnerabilities are constantly being identified and most vendors will offer security patches to address these issues in a timely manner. These vulnerabilities will be exploited if not patched, which is why this requirement insists on applying patches within a month from when they are made available by the software vendor. Of course, the sooner they are applied, the less likelihood of the vulnerability in question being exploited.

6.2 *Establish a process to identify newly discovered security vulnerabilities (for example, subscribe to alert services freely available on the Internet). Update standards to address new vulnerability issues.*

This standard has two components that are required in order to achieve successful compliance with PCI DSS. First, the business must develop a process to identify newly discovered vulnerabilities. There are a number of alert notification resources available, both free and fee-based. In addition, many technology vendors offer these types of services for their own products. Please see the Resources section for some common vulnerability alert notification resources. It is recommended to subscribe to several of these services, since sometimes there is variation in the content and timeliness of the actual alert notification. Organizations must also remember to keep abreast of alert notifications for all levels of the cardholder data environment. In other words, the organization should subscribe to alert notification services for all of the critical technologies (e.g., firewall, IDS/IPS, operating systems, vendor applications, etc.) that are supporting the cardholder data environment.

Second, in order to comply with this standard, organizations must develop standards to address newly identified vulnerability issues. These standards should be customized to meet organization-specific requirements, but at a minimum they should address any newly identified vulnerabilities. Furthermore, organizational standards must be regularly updated to address new vulnerability issues.

Although the vulnerability landscape is ever-changing, organizations must be both diligent and proactive in order to address any potential risk to the cardholder data environment in a timely manner. The only way to do this is to have formalized business processes and procedures in place that will enable organizations to quickly identify and respond to newly discovered security vulnerabilities. It is recommended that organizations include in their vulnerability management programs both immediate and planned response procedures for newly identified vulnerabilities. The organization should design, implement, and manage a risk-based program to appropriately deal with newly identified vulnerabilities. Vulnerabilities that are determined to be critical in nature must be addressed immediately. Other vulnerabilities, while still important to the overall protection of the cardholder data environment, may be better addressed on a planned and routine vulnerability management cycle.

6.3 *Develop software applications based on industry best practices and incorporate information security throughout the software development life cycle.*

In Chapter 2 we discussed the System Development Life Cycle (SDLC) and security's role through the life cycle. As discussed, SDLC is the formalized methodology and process used to develop applications. Using industry best practices enables organizations to develop applications that are secure and based on well-tested techniques. When best practices are utilized correctly, applications are less prone to common attacks and vulnerabilities. When security is not interwoven into the entire process, the application is vulnerable to a number of threats. When security is managed proactively, rather than as an afterthought, it is both more effective and less costly. There are many security-based strategies that provide strong security controls with a low cost if they are properly aligned with all of the phases of the SDLC.

6.3.1 *Testing of all security patches and system and software configuration changes before deployment.*

Although security patches are intended to maintain and protect systems from newly identified vulnerabilities, they must be tested in case the effects of their deployment could have unintended consequences. The new release could inadvertently cause functional problems at the application level or actually create additional vulnerabilities. It is also important to remember that, to be effective, the testing environment must be identical to production conditions. If the two environments do not resemble each other, then the security patch could appear to work in the test environment but still cause significant problems with the production cardholder data environment.

6.3.2 *Separate development, test, and production environments.*

This PCI DSS requirement provides protection by segregating three key phases of system development (development, testing, and production). These environments must be separated in order to build and maintain secure systems and applications. By commingling data among the different phases of system and application development, or by simply "promoting" an environment (i.e., promoting the development environment to the testing environment, or the testing environment to the production environment, instead of keeping them as separate, discrete environments), organizations significantly increase the security risk to their cardholder data environment.

Another benefit to keeping these three environments separate is that, should the need for any system enhancements arise, they can be developed and tested in environments that mirror the production environment without interrupting it.

6.3.3 *Separation of duties between development, test, and production environments.*

Separation, or segregation, of duties is an industry best practice–based security control that must be successfully implemented and maintained for PCI DSS compliance. The intent of the standard is to have an appropriate level of control over the organization's various cardholder data environments. In addition to the separation of duties, it is recommended to have formalized process controls with management approval and sign-off as the organization progresses through the development, test, and production environments, with the sign-offs indicating that performance in each environment has met the expected requirements.

6.3.4 *Production data (live PANs) are not used for testing or development.*

Most testing and development environments tend to be less secure, and it is possible that users that would not normally have access to sensitive cardholder data would be participating in the review of the development and testing environments (such as quality assurance [QA] teams or developers). Because of this, production data should not be used in the test or development environments, as it creates a substantial risk by allowing unauthorized users access to otherwise protected data. This goes back to the concept of Least Privileged Access Control—users should have access only to that information which is required to effectively perform their jobs. In this instance, it is not necessary for developers or QA team member to have access to the sensitive cardholder data in order to effectively do their jobs.

6.3.5 *Removal of test data and accounts before production systems become active.*

PCI DSS requirement 6.3.5 addresses the need to ensure that test data and accounts are removed from systems before moving into production. As recently discussed, although a production system will need to be tested, the users testing it will not necessarily get access to the system once it is production ready. Hence, the IDs they were using to access the environment should be removed.

As far as removing the test data, this is a common best practice, as a production environment should have production data only. Having any non-production data in a production environment can result in skewed reports, data analytics, and so on.

6.3.6 *Removal of custom application accounts, usernames, and passwords before applications become active or are released to customers.*

Remember, the premise of PCI DSS 6.3 requires organizations to develop software applications based on industry best practices and to incorporate information security throughout the SDLC. PCI DSS requirement 6.3.6 specifically addresses accounts, user names, and password components before applications are placed into production. During the SDLC, many developers insert accounts, user names, and passwords into the application as part of the development process. Since this practice is generally required in the development phase, these components (accounts, user names, and passwords) must be removed before an application is deployed into production. If these components are not removed, attackers can leverage these access points as part of their attack methodology.

6.3.7 *Review of custom code prior to release to production or customers in order to identify any potential coding vulnerability.*

PCI DSS requirement 6.4 relates to change control. Change control is an invaluable protective measure that is utilized to develop and maintain secure systems and applications. At its highest level, its main goals are to apply changes with minimal disruption to production services and reduce the need to back out any changes by requiring that all changes be tested in a non-production environment that mirrors the production environment. Without a good change-control policy, organizations run the risk of introducing unnecessary changes and new defects to a production environment. At a minimum, a change control policy should require that:

- Analysis is performed to determine the priority of the change being requested.
- Analysis is performed to identify any possible risks to applying the change to the existing customer environment.
- Once the change is approved, all documentation related to the environment is applied to be updated.
- The change must be thoroughly tested prior to being applied to the production environment.
- Regression testing must be performed to ensure the change does not affect any other functions currently working as designed.

Now that we have a general understanding of change control, let us examine the specific requirements for PCI DSS.

6.4 *Follow change control procedures for all system and software configuration changes. The procedures must include the following.*

6.4.1 *Documentation of impact.*

The first step of the change management process is to appropriately document the impact of the proposed change. Prior to implementing the actual change, clearly documenting the change and any associated impact offers a transparent and high-level view of the change and its impact on the cardholder data environment. This information must be reviewed before initializing any changes. Management approval and sign-off (the next phase of change control) is difficult to achieve if management does not have a clear picture (including the associated impact and risk) of the change they are being asked to approve.

6.4.2 *Management sign-off by appropriate parties.*

This step in the change control process ensures that management has been properly communicated to and accepts responsibility for any possible negative impacts to the cardholder data environment as a result of the change being made.

6.4.3 *Testing of operational functionality.*

In a perfect world, all system changes go as planned and do not have any unintended consequences. However, this is not always the case, and organizations must take a proactive approach and validate their change management plan as much as possible before actually implementing the change. Testing is the way to ensure the change will function as planned. The test must be performed to simulate the actual change and be done in an environment that replicates the production environment. Any differences, even those that appear insignificant, can have a surprisingly large impact on the production environment. Properly performed testing (i.e., performed in a test environment that fully replicates the production environment) should indicate any potential problems before the actual change is made. Since there are some cases where production problems have occurred, even after comprehensive testing, back-out procedures must be incorporated into the change control procedures. In addition to testing that a change performs as expected based on its requirements, it is essential that all other functions in the system are tested as well, to ensure that the application of the change has not negatively impacted their expected behavior.

6.4.4 *Back-out procedures.*

Back-out procedures are the steps taken when problems occur in the production environment after a change has been implemented. The intent is to return the production environment to the last known stable and operable configuration, prior to the change being implemented.

The vast improvement in Web-based technologies has caused many businesses to depend on these technologies as part of routine payment card transactions. PCI DSS requirement 6.5 addresses the use of these technologies. Despite the numerous benefits of Web-based technologies, there are substantial risks that organizations face if they do not protect themselves from the known and inherent risks associated with Web-based applications. It is important to note that some of the more common reasons for using Web-based applications (e.g., ease of use, accessibility to customers over the Internet) are the same reasons for the associated risks and security vulnerabilities. Fortunately, many of the common vulnerabilities can be addressed by following best practices and tightening controls around web applications. Specifically, the Open Web Application Security Project (OWASP) is an invaluable resource to address these issues. OWASP is best described by its mission statement:

"The Open Web Application Security Project (OWASP) is a worldwide free and open community focused on improving the security of application software. Our mission is to make application security 'visible,' so that people and organizations can make informed decisions about application security risks. Everyone is free to participate in OWASP and all of our materials are available under an open source license. The OWASP Foundation is a 501c3 not-for-profit charitable organization that ensures the ongoing availability and support for our work."

The following information specifically addresses the Web-application and security concerns from the PCI DSS–requirements perspective and uses information from

OWASP's Web site www.owasp.org (since OWASP is specifically mentioned in the standard) to address each and offers some of their suggestions on how an organization can protect itself. However, for additional information, readers are strongly encouraged to visit OWASP's Web site at www.owasp.org.

6.5 *Develop all web applications based on secure coding guidelines such as the Open Web Application Security Project guidelines. Review custom application code to identify coding vulnerabilities. Cover prevention of common coding vulnerabilities in software development processes, to include the following.*

6.5.1 *Unvalidated input.*

According to OWASP:

> "Web applications use input from HTTP requests (and occasionally files) to determine how to respond. Attackers can tamper with any part of an HTTP request, including the url querystring, headers, cookies, form fields, and hidden fields, to try to bypass the site's security mechanisms. Common names for common input tampering attacks include: forced browsing, command insertion, cross site scripting, buffer overflows, format string attacks, SQL injection, cookie poisoning, and hidden field manipulation."

To avoid falling victim to an input tampering attack, OWASP suggests that organizations ensure that all input parameters are validated and checked against the specifications of what has been determined as acceptable input.

6.5.2 *Broken access control (for example, malicious use of user IDs).*

In various sections of this book, we have discussed access control and its role in protecting the security cardholder data. In order to avoid the harm that can result from broken access control, OWASP suggests the use of an access control matrix in order to manage the access control rules to reduce the risk of any issues, and also the use of extensive testing of the access control mechanism. The access control matrix will serve as easy-to-reference documentation that lists exactly which users and groups have what access to an environment. Extensive testing will ensure that the requirements are met and not easily circumvented by means such as path traversal (where a hacker obtains the URL to a document or page they would normally not have access to and pastes it into a Web browser without having to authenticate themselves because they have bypassed the screen that would ask for authentication).

6.5.3 *Broken authentication and session management (use of account credentials and session cookies).*

In various sections of this book, we have discussed the importance of authentication, the benefits of using multiples methods of authentication versus a single method of authentication, and authentication's role in protecting cardholder data. However, as OWASP points out, even solid authentication practices can be flawed and compromise the security of the cardholder data environment. Some examples include:

- A user properly accesses the environment but walks away from their workstation. Another person takes the user's place and is able to access the data within the environment because reauthentication is not required (since the user's session is still valid).
- A malicious user wants to gain access to the cardholder data environment using a valid user's ID but does not know the user's password. However, the valid user has indicated that they want their personal workstation to remember the password whenever the valid user name is entered.

In some cases, requiring the use of more than one authentication method (i.e., a password and a fingerprint) can help reduce the risk of broken authentication and session management. But, as OWASP suggests, organizations should develop a policy that includes the critical errors listed in Exhibit 5.2.

Critical Area	Description (from OWASP)
Password Strength	Passwords should have restrictions that require a minimum size and complexity for the password. Complexity typically requires the use of minimum combinations of alphabetic, numeric, and/or non-alphanumeric characters in a user's password (e.g., at least one of each). Users should be required to change their password periodically. Users should be prevented from reusing previous passwords.
Password Use	Users should be restricted to a defined number of login attempts per unit of time, and repeated failed login attempts should be logged. Passwords provided during failed login attempts should not be recorded, as this may expose a user's password to whoever can gain access to this log. The system should not indicate whether it was the username or password that was wrong if a login attempt fails. Users should be informed of the date/time of their last successful login and the number of failed access attempts to their account since that time.
Password Change Controls	A single password change mechanism should be used wherever users are allowed to change a password, regardless of the situation. Users should always be required to provide both their old and new password when changing their password (like all account information). If forgotten passwords are emailed to users, the system should require the user to reauthenticate whenever the user is changing their email address. Otherwise an attacker who temporarily has access to their session (e.g., by walking up to their computer while they are logged in) can simply change their email address and request a "forgotten" password be mailed to them.
Password Storage	All passwords must be stored in either hashed or encrypted form to protect them from exposure, regardless of where they are stored. Hashed form is preferred since it is not reversible. Encryption should be used when the plaintext password is needed, such as when using the password to login to another system. Passwords should never be hardcoded in any source code. Decryption keys must be strongly protected to ensure that they cannot be grabbed and used to decrypt the password file.
Protecting Credentials in Transit	The only effective technique is to encrypt the entire login transaction using something like SSL. Simple transformations of the password, such as hashing it on the client prior to transmission, provide little protection, as the hashed version can simply be intercepted and retransmitted even though the actual plaintext password might not be known.

Session ID Protection	Ideally, a user's entire session should be protected via SSL. If this is done, then the session ID (e.g., session cookie) cannot be grabbed off the network, which is the biggest risk of exposure for a session ID. If SSL is not viable for performance or other reasons then session IDs themselves must be protected in other ways. First, they should never be included in the URL, as they can be cached by the browser, sent in the referrer header, or accidentally forwarded to a "friend." Session IDs should be long, complicated, random numbers that cannot be easily guessed. Session IDs can also be changed frequently during a session to reduce how long a session ID is valid. Session IDs must be changed when switching to SSL, authenticating, or enacting other major transitions. Session IDs chosen by a user should never be accepted.
Account Lists	Systems should be designed to avoid allowing users to gain access to a list of the account names on the site. If lists of users must be presented, it is recommended that some form of pseudonym (screen name) that maps to the actual account be listed instead. That way the pseudonym cannot be used during a login attempt or some other hack that goes after a user's account.
Browser Caching	Authentication and session data should never be submitted as part of a GET; POST should always be used instead. Authentication pages should be marked with all varieties of the no-cache tag to prevent someone from using the back button in a user's browser to back up to the login page and resubmit the previously typed-in credentials. Many browsers now support the autocomplete=false flag to prevent storing of credentials in autocomplete caches.
Trust Relationships	Your site architecture should avoid implicit trust between components whenever possible. Each component should authenticate itself to any other component it is interacting with unless there is a strong reason not to (such as performance or lack of a usable mechanism). If trust relationships are required, strong procedural and architecture mechanisms should be in place to ensure that such trust cannot be abused as the site architecture evolves over time.

EXHIBIT 5.2. From OWASP: Critical Areas to Include in an Authentication Policy

6.5.4 *Cross-site scripting (XSS) attacks.*
According to OWASP:

"Cross-site scripting (XSS) attacks occur when an attacker uses a web application to send malicious code, generally in the form of a browser side script, to a different end user. Flaws that allow these attacks to succeed are quite widespread and occur anywhere a web application uses input from a user in the output it generates without validating or encoding it.

"An attacker can use XSS to send malicious script to an unsuspecting user. The end user's browser has no way to know that the script should not be trusted, and will execute the script. Because it thinks the script came from a trusted source, the malicious script can access any cookies, session tokens, or other sensitive information retained by your browser and used with that site. These scripts can even rewrite the content of the HTML page.

. . .

"The best way to protect a web application from XSS attacks is ensure that your application performs validation of all headers, cookies, query strings, form fields, and hidden fields (i.e., all parameters) against a rigorous specification of what should be allowed. The validation should not attempt to identify active content and remove, filter, or sanitize it. There are too many types of active content and too many ways of encoding it to get around filters for such content. We strongly recommend a 'positive' security policy that specifies what is allowed. 'Negative' or attack signature based policies are difficult to maintain and are likely to be incomplete."

6.5.5 *Buffer overflows.*
According to OWASP:

"Buffer overflow is probably the best known form of software security vulnerability. Most software developers know what a buffer overflow vulnerability is, but buffer overflow attacks against both legacy and newly-developed applications are still quite common. Part of the problem is due to the wide variety of ways buffer overflows can occur, and part is due to the error-prone techniques often used to prevent them.

"Buffer overflows are not easy to discover and even when one is discovered, it is generally extremely difficult to exploit. Nevertheless, attackers have managed to identify buffer overflows in a staggering array of products and components."

To protect themselves, organizations should keep abreast of the latest bug reports, be sure to always apply the latest patches, and scan their Web site regularly to look for buffer overflow flaws.

6.5.6 *Injection flaws (for example, structured query language (SQL) injection).*

According to OWASP:

"Injection flaws allow attackers to relay malicious code through a web application to another system. These attacks include calls to the operating system via system calls, the use of external programs via shell commands, as well as calls to backend databases via SQL (i.e., SQL injection). Whole scripts written in perl, python, and other languages can be injected into poorly designed web applications and executed. Any time a web application uses an interpreter of any type there is a danger of an injection attack.

. . .

"The simplest way to protect against injection is to avoid accessing external interpreters wherever possible. For many shell commands and some system calls, there are language specific libraries that perform the same functions. Using such libraries does not involve the operating system shell interpreter, and therefore avoids a large number of problems with shell commands."

6.5.7 *Improper error handling.*
    According to OWASP:

"Improper handling of errors can introduce a variety of security problems for a web site. The most common problem is when detailed internal error messages such as stack traces, database dumps, and error codes are displayed to the user (hacker). These messages reveal implementation details that should never be revealed. Such details can provide hackers important clues on potential flaws in the site and such messages are also disturbing to normal users.

"Web applications frequently generate error conditions during normal operation. Out of memory, null pointer exceptions, system call failure, database unavailable, network timeout, and hundreds of other common conditions can cause errors to be generated. These errors must be handled according to a well thought out scheme that will provide a meaningful error message to the user, diagnostic information to the site maintainers, and no useful information to an attacker.

. . .

"A specific policy for how to handle errors should be documented, including the types of errors to be handled and for each, what information is going to be reported back to the user, and what information is going to be logged. All developers need to understand the policy and ensure that their code follows it.

"In the implementation, ensure that the site is built to gracefully handle all possible errors. When errors occur, the site should respond with a specifically designed result that is helpful to the user without revealing unnecessary internal details. Certain classes of errors should be logged to help detect implementation flaws in the site and/or hacking attempts. Very few sites have any intrusion detection capabilities in their web application, but it is certainly conceivable that a web application could track repeated failed attempts and generate alerts. Note that the vast majority of web application attacks are never detected because so few sites have the capability to detect them. Therefore, the prevalence of web application security attacks is likely to be seriously underestimated."

6.5.8 *Insecure storage.*

According to OWASP:

"Most web applications have a need to store sensitive information, either in a database or on a file system somewhere. The information might be passwords, credit card numbers, account records, or proprietary information. Frequently, encryption techniques are used to protect this sensitive information. While encryption has become relatively easy to implement and use, developers still frequently make mistakes while integrating it into a web application. Developers may overestimate the protection gained by using encryption and not be as careful in securing other aspects of the site.

A few areas where mistakes are commonly made include:

■ Failure to encrypt critical data
■ Insecure storage of keys, certificates, and passwords
■ Improper storage of secrets in memory
■ Poor sources of randomness
■ Poor choice of algorithm
■ Attempting to invent a new encryption algorithm
■ Failure to include support for encryption key changes and other required maintenance procedures

. . .

"The easiest way to protect against cryptographic flaws is to minimize the use of encryption and only keep information that is absolutely necessary. For example, rather than encrypting credit card numbers and storing them, simply require users to re-enter the numbers. Also, instead of storing encrypted passwords, use a one way function, such as SHA-1, to hash the passwords."

6.5.9 *Denial of service.*

According to OWASP:

"A web application can't easily tell the difference between an attack and ordinary traffic. There are many factors that contribute to this difficulty, but one of the most important is that, for a number of reasons, IP addresses are not useful as an identification credential. Because there is no reliable way to tell where an HTTP request is from, it is very difficult to filter out malicious traffic. For distributed attacks, how would an application tell the difference between a true attack, multiple users all hitting reload at the same time (which might happen if there is a temporary problem with the site), or getting 'slashdotted'?

"Most web servers can handle several hundred concurrent users under normal use. A single attacker can generate enough traffic from a single host to swamp many applications. Load balancing can make these attacks more difficult, but far from impossible, especially if sessions are tied to a particular server. This is a good reason to make an application's session data as small as possible and to make it somewhat difficult to start a new session.

. . .

"Defending against denial of service attacks is difficult, as there is no way to protect against these attacks perfectly. As a general rule, you should limit the resources allocated to any user to a bare minimum. For authenticated users, it is possible to establish quotas so that you can limit the amount of load a particular user can put on your system. In particular, you might consider only handling one request per user at a time by synchronizing on the user's session. You might also consider dropping any requests that you are currently processing for a user when another request from that user arrives.

"For unauthenticated users, you should avoid any unnecessary access to databases or other expensive resources. Try to architect the flow of your site so that an unauthenticated user will not be able to invoke any expensive operations. You might consider caching the content received by unauthenticated users instead of generating it or accessing databases to retrieve it.

"You should also check your error handling scheme to ensure that an error cannot affect the overall operation of the application."

6.5.10 *Insecure configuration management.*
According to OWASP:

"There are a wide variety of server configuration problems that can plague the security of a site. These include:

- Unpatched security flaws in the server software
- Server software flaws or misconfigurations that permit directory listing and directory traversal attacks
- Unnecessary default, backup, or sample files, including scripts, applications, configuration files, and web pages
- Improper file and directory permissions
- Unnecessary services enabled, including content management and remote administration
- Default accounts with their default passwords
- Administrative or debugging functions that are enabled or accessible
- Overly informative error messages (more details in the error handling section)
- Misconfigured SSL certificates and encryption settings
- Use of self-signed certificates to achieve authentication and man-in-the-middle protection
- Use of default certificates
- Improper authentication with external systems

"Some of these problems can be detected with readily available security scanning tools. Once detected, these problems can be easily exploited and result in total compromise of a website. Successful attacks can also result in the compromise of backend systems including databases and corporate networks. Having secure software and a secure configuration are both required in order to have a secure site.

. . .

"The first step is to create a hardening guideline for your particular web server and application server configuration. This configuration should be used on all hosts running the application and in the development environment as well. We recommend starting with any existing guidance you can find from your vendor or those available from the various existing security organizations such as OWASP, CERT, and SANS and then tailoring them for your particular needs. The hardening guideline should include the following topics:

- Configuring all security mechanisms
- Turning off all unused services
- Setting up roles, permissions, and accounts, including disabling all default accounts or changing their passwords
- Logging and alerts

"Once your guideline has been established, use it to configure and maintain your servers. If you have a large number of servers to configure, consider semi-automating or completely automating the configuration process. Use an existing configuration tool or develop your own. A number of such tools already exist. You can also use disk replication tools such as Ghost to take an image of an existing hardened server, and then replicate that image to new servers. Such a process may or may not work for you given your particular environment.

"Keeping the server configuration secure requires vigilance. You should be sure that the responsibility for keeping the server configuration up to date is assigned to an individual or team. The maintenance process should include:

- Monitoring the latest security vulnerabilities published
- Applying the latest security patches
- Updating the security configuration guideline
- Regular vulnerability scanning from both internal and external perspectives
- Regular internal reviews of the server's security configuration as compared to your configuration guide
- Regular status reports to upper management documenting overall security posture"

6.6 *Ensure that all web-facing applications are protected against known attacks by applying either of the following methods:*
- *Having all custom application code reviewed for common vulnerabilities by an organization that specializes in application security*
- *Installing an application layer firewall in front of web-facing applications.*

Note: This method is considered a best practice until June 30, 2008, after which it becomes a requirement.

In order to be compliant with PCI DSS requirement 6.6, organizations must take specific measures to address known attacks and vulnerabilities associated with Web-facing applications. Web-facing applications typically pose substantial risk to the cardholder data environment since they are vulnerable to the Internet and all of its potential threats.

The requirement offers two acceptable safeguards for this situation. However, it is important to note that the second control *(Installing an application layer firewall in front of web-facing applications)* is currently considered a best practice but will be a mandatory requirement after June 30, 2008.

Following the first safeguard, all custom application code must be reviewed for common vulnerabilities by an organization that specializes in application security. This requirement is relatively straightforward and the protection to the cardholder data environment is offered by having an objective third party with specialized skills review your organization's custom application for common vulnerabilities.

The second safeguard offers protection by having an application layer firewall in front of your organization's Web-facing application. Application layer firewalls improve the overall security of the Web-facing application by preventing attacks that are likely to occur based on common attacks that Web-facing applications are likely to face. This application layer firewall offers another layer of defense between the Internet (and all of its associated risks) and your organization's cardholder data environment.

CHAPTER 6

Implement Strong Access Control Measures

This chapter reviews the Payment Card Industry Data Security Standards (PCI DSS) requirements that mandate access control requirements to the cardholder data environment. Broadly, these requirements dictate that only those persons who need access to the cardholder data environment in order to effectively complete their job requirements should be granted access to the cardholder data environment. A more detailed review of the requirements discusses the fact that, for those persons who are granted access, PCI DSS sets forth specific requirements regarding the extent of their access and how the individual is given access (i.e., user name and password requirements). Organizations will need to obtain a comprehensive understanding of access control because it is pivotal to PCI DSS compliance. Remember that cardholder data is an invaluable asset—controlling who, how, and why it is accessed—is essential.

REQUIREMENT 7: RESTRICT ACCESS TO CARDHOLDER DATA BY BUSINESS NEED TO KNOW

This requirement ensures critical data can only be accessed by authorized personnel.

As discussed in Chapter 2, the concept of Least Privileged Access Control (sometimes referred to as *need to know*) is the cornerstone of many security controls. In summary, access should be strictly controlled and only provided to those who must have it to perform their specific job requirements.

7.1 *Limit access to computing resources and cardholder information only to those individuals whose job requires such access.*

This requirement is based on the principle that the fewer number of individuals who have access to sensitive data, the less likely a violation of PCI DSS is to occur.

7.2 *Establish a mechanism for systems with multiple users that restricts access based on a user's need to know and is set to "deny all" unless specifically allowed.*

This is a technical control that actually enforces the concept of Least Privileged Access Control. Systems that have multiple users must be configured in a manner in which all users do not have the same level of access, with each individual's access being appropriate to their specific job responsibilities. In other words, just because a system is capable of supporting multiple users, that does not mean that all of the system's users should have the ability to access information equally.

REQUIREMENT 8: ASSIGN A UNIQUE ID TO EACH PERSON WITH COMPUTER ACCESS

Assigning a unique identification (ID) to each person with [computer] access ensures that actions taken on critical data and systems are performed by, and can be traced to, known and authorized users.

8.1 *Identify all users with a unique user name before allowing them to access system components or cardholder data.*

The assignment of unique IDs to all system users prior to enabling user access is essential. Without the ability to uniquely identify a user in a system, it is impossible to hold that user accountable for their actions within the system.

8.2 *In addition to assigning a unique ID, employ at least one of the following methods to authenticate all users:*

- *Password*
- *Token devices (e.g., SecureID, certificates, or public key)*
- *Biometrics.*

As authentication was discussed in Chapter 2, we will just emphasize a few key points that are essential to this particular PCI DSS requirement. Authentication (something you know, have, or are) in conjunction with a unique ID is critical to managing system user security. Additionally, the more authentication methods employed by the organization, the less likely that a breach of the secured data environment will occur. For example, although the use of a unique user ID in conjunction with a password is considered to be in compliance with this requirement, a data environment that requires an additional biometrics authentication method (i.e., the use of a fingerprint) in order to gain access is less likely to be compromised.

8.3 *Implement two-factor authentication for remote access to the network by employees, administrators, and third parties. Use technologies such as remote authentication and dial-in service (RADIUS) or terminal access controller access control system (TACACS) with tokens; or VPN (based on SSL/TLS/TLS or IPSEC) with individual certificates.*

Since two-factor authentication provides a stronger level of security over single-factor (as mentioned in the analysis of requirement 8.2 above), it must be used for authentication scenarios that pose greater risks to the cardholder data environment, such as accessing the information remotely.

8.4 *Encrypt all passwords during transmission and storage on all system components.*

Since the password is an essential component for logical access control, it must be properly protected at all times. The best protection method for securing passwords is to encrypt the password during transmission and storage. Many of the encryption key–management principles and practices should also be applied to the encryption of passwords.

PCI DSS requirement 8.5 details a number of detailed requirements regarding nonconsumer (user and administrator specific)–based authentication and password management practices.

8.5 *Ensure proper user authentication and password management for non-consumer users and administrators on all system components as follows:*

8.5.1 *Control addition, deletion, and modification of user IDs, credentials, and other identifier objects.*

System-identifying objects, user IDs, and credentials should be carefully controlled or managed, and only necessary and authorized additions, deletions, and modifications should be allowed. One of the easier ways to control this is to narrowly limit the number of people who have the ability to add, delete, and modify these objects. This will not only help to ensure compliance with this specific requirement, but will also help to control who has access to the cardholder data environment.

8.5.2 *Verify user identity before performing password resets.*

The intent of this requirement is to ensure that an unauthorized user does not have the opportunity to maliciously use a valid user ID by requesting a password change for a user ID that does not belong to them. For example, if an unauthorized person was able to acquire a user ID, he could then request a password reset and be able to access the cardholder data environment under false pretenses. Properly verifying a user's identity before performing a password reset prevents this type of malicious activity.

8.5.3 *Set first-time passwords to a unique value for each user and change immediately after the first use.*

This is an information security best practice to prevent account and password abuse. If the same password were issued for every user, it would not take very long for malicious users to learn that password. In conjunction with a user ID account, this information could be leveraged for a malicious attack. The password should also be required to be changed to a strong password (i.e., one that requires a combination of alpha and numeric characters or the use of at least one "special" character) that only the user knows. Even if each user is issued a unique password, the possibility still exists that someone other than the user will know what the password is or be able to guess it.

8.5.4 *Immediately revoke access for any terminated users.*

This requirement is relatively straightforward. After a relationship with an organization has been terminated, they no longer have a legitimate business need for system access. PCI DSS requirement 8.5.4 emphasizes that system access should be immediately disabled. Unfortunately, there have been many organizations that fall victim to malicious acts performed by recently terminated employees. Depending on the circumstances of the employee's termination, the employee may respond negatively and attempt to damage the organization. There are also cases where the former employee has accessed proprietary or otherwise sensitive information and shared that information with their new employer. The information could even be leveraged in the committing of a criminal act. Regardless of the circumstances surrounding an employee's departure, access should be revoked as soon as it is no longer needed. Even if an employee leaves on good terms (or your organization defines *termination* as meaning that an employee is no longer associated with the organization, regardless of circumstances), access to cardholder data must immediately be removed.

8.5.5 *Remove inactive user accounts at least every 90 days.*

Ideally, inactive accounts are removed as soon as it is determined they are no longer required. However, there are some legitimate business reasons that prevent the removal from occurring immediately. Additionally, many user accounts are not needed on a daily basis and it may be difficult to determine exactly when they are no longer needed. This control acts as a fail-safe to ensure that if an account has remained inactive for 90 days, it must be removed.

8.5.6 *Enable accounts used by vendors for remote maintenance only during the time period needed.*

It is understandable and common practice that outside vendors will periodically be required to perform remote system maintenance. However, this does not mean vendors should have unrestricted access. Access should be granted only for the exact duration required for the vendor to complete the maintenance tasks. Once the task has been completed, system access must be immediately revoked.

8.5.7 *Communicate password procedures and policies to all users who have access to cardholder data.*

This is a seemingly simple yet highly important security control. Proper communication and awareness of password procedures and policies strengthen the organizations security posture and ensure that users are held accountable for compliance with the organization's password procedures and policies. In other words, employees cannot comply with policies and procedures they are not aware of.

8.5.8 *Do not use group, shared, or generic accounts and passwords.*

The use of group, shared, or generic accounts and passwords prevents individual accountability. As previously discussed, individual accountability is an invaluable PCI DSS requirement that strengthens the organization's overall security posture. Additionally, it is necessary for successful incident response and investigation. This level of detail allows organizations to determine who did or did not perform actions within the cardholder data environment.

8.5.9 *Change user passwords at least every 90 days.*

This control is one of many password best practices that must be implemented to reduce the likelihood of inappropriate use of passwords. The greater the frequency of password changes, the less likely the password will be compromised. In other words, the shorter the duration of time the same password is allowed to be used, the less chance there is that an unauthorized individual will obtain the password.

8.5.10 *Require a minimum password length of at least seven characters.*

This password control is utilized to increase the complexity of the password and reduce the likelihood that it can be compromised by a "brute force" attack or similar method. A brute force attack is deployed to discover or "guess" a user's password. The attack continuously attempts to decipher the password by randomly submitting password characters in an attempt to access the account. The increased length of the password significantly increases the difficulty of a password compromise.

8.5.11 *Use passwords containing both numeric and alphabetic characters.*

PCI DSS requirement 8.5.11 closely aligns with requirement 8.5.10 and is intended to increase the complexity of passwords in order to increase the difficulty of, or otherwise deter, a password attack. Similar to the protection offered by increased password length safeguards, alphanumeric complexity significantly increases the overall strength of the password.

8.5.12 *Do not allow an individual to submit a new password that is the same as any of the last four passwords he or she has used.*

PCI DSS requirement 8.5.12 is a security control intended to reduce the risk of unauthorized password use. If authorized systems users are allowed to recycle passwords, the likelihood of unauthorized password use is substantially increased. The longer the duration of cycle time between passwords' reuse, the smaller the window of opportunity for password abuse by unauthorized system users. Allowing an authorized user to stay with the same password over an extended period of time yields the same risks as not changing the password as stipulated under PCI DSS requirement 8.5.9.

8.5.13 *Limit repeated access attempts by locking out the user ID after not more than six attempts.*

The intent of PCI DSS requirement 8.5.13 is to prevent brute force attacks (as described in PCI DSS 8.5.10). The protection offered by this control is that unsuccessful repeated access attempts are likely indicative of a brute force attack. After six unsuccessful access attempts, the user ID must be locked out. This action reduces the window of opportunity for attack. Furthermore, if an authorized user cannot access the system within six attempts, then it is likely they have forgotten their password and it will be required to reset it anyway.

8.5.14 *Set the lockout duration to thirty minutes or until administrator enables the user ID.*

The security protection for PCI DSS requirement 8.5.14 also prevents brute force attacks. If a session remains locked out, the attacker will likely realize that they will not be able to access the user ID and will give up the attack. If a legitimate user needs the account unlocked sooner than 30 minutes, requiring a system administrator to validate that the user is legitimate ensures that an unauthorized user will not gain access to the account.

8.5.15 *If a session has been idle for more than 15 minutes, require the user to re-enter the password to re-activate the terminal.*

This control also offers protection to the cardholder data environment by reducing the window of opportunity for unauthorized system access. Session inactivity beyond 15 minutes likely indicates that the authorized user no longer requires an "open" session. The longer an inactive session remains open, the greater the risk that an unauthorized user will access the system under the guise of a legitimate user session. By requiring the user to reenter their password after an idle session, the organization is increasing security to the cardholder data environment by increasing the strength of access controls.

8.5.16 *Authenticate all access to any database containing cardholder data. This includes access by applications, administrators, and all other users.*

Chapter 2 offers a detailed discussion of authentication. For PCI DSS requirement 8.5.16, the takeaway is that organizations must authenticate all access to any database containing cardholder data. It is important to note that the requirement emphasizes all access and clearly denotes access by applications, administrators, and all other users. Since the contents of a database containing cardholder data is an invaluable organizational asset (and the primary reason PCI DSS protections are implemented), all sources (applications, administrators, and all other users) requesting access must be properly authenticated.

REQUIREMENT 9: RESTRICT PHYSICAL ACCESS TO CARDHOLDER DATA

Any physical access to data or systems that house cardholder data provides the opportunity for individuals to access devices or data and to remove systems or hardcopies, and should be appropriately restricted.

Physical security is the first layer of defense when utilizing a defense-in-depth approach to protecting the cardholder data environment. When physical security is effectively managed with logical and administrative security controls, it offers strong layers of protection for the cardholder data environment. As with all the components of an effective information security and data protection program, this control is only as effective as its weakest link. Organizations are heading down the wrong path when they are looking for a one-size-fits-all approach to security. No one part of PCI DSS is stronger or more important than any other part. The intelligent view is to approach the controls as specific tactics that are woven together to offer increased levels of data protection. For example, the best firewall configuration in the world does not offer any benefits of PCI DSS compliance if an unauthorized individual, with malicious intent, can walk right into the cardholder data environment and steal sensitive cardholder data. Conversely, the latest and greatest physical security controls are useless, if the organization does not have any logical access controls and appropriate protections over their internal network. The right approach is for organizations to design, implement, and manage physical security controls that are appropriate to their specific organization and complement logical and administrative security controls. The primer on physical security from Chapter 2 covers the intent and common criteria required for a successful physical security implementation. The following information details the PCI DSS requirements and any additional notes that may be useful to achieving PCI DSS compliance.

9.1 *Use appropriate facility entry controls to limit and monitor physical access to systems that store, process, or transmit cardholder data.*

The phrase *appropriate* is open to interpretation, varies from organization to organization, and is dependent on a number of organization-specific factors (e.g., geography, building architecture, security technology, etc.), but organizations are ultimately responsible for designing, implementing, and managing controls that limit and monitor physical access to systems that store, process, or transmit cardholder data.

Although comprehensive details regarding physical security are outside the scope of PCI DSS, the following requirements address the minimum recommendations that organizations must incorporate into their information security program.

9.1.1 *Use cameras to monitor sensitive areas. Audit collected data and correlate with other entries. Store for at least three months, unless otherwise restricted by law.*

Depending on how they are utilized by an organization, surveillance cameras can offer a variety of security controls. First, when placed in a visible location they act as a deterrent to the potential attacker. People will think twice about attacking the cardholder data environment if they believe they are being monitored. Second, if cameras are monitored in real time they can alert the organization to inappropriate behavior or attack and allow organizations to respond before an incident occurs. Even if the cameras are not monitored in real time, they can still be an invaluable investigative tool. Personnel investigating an incident can review the tapes to find out additional information (time, date, attackers description, etc.) surrounding a security breach.

9.1.2 *Restrict physical access to publicly accessible network jacks.*

Since network jacks are a potential gateway (into the cardholder data environment) their physical security must be protected. If appropriate physical safeguards are not in place, it is too easy for a malicious person to plug into the network and access payment card and otherwise protected information from the cardholder data environment.

9.1.3 *Restrict physical access to wireless access points, gateways, and handheld devices.*

In our discussion of wireless security in Chapter 2, we discovered that wireless access points, gateways, and handheld devices are highly vulnerable gateways to the cardholder data environment that can be easily exploited by attackers if not properly physically secured. PCI DSS requirement 9.1.3 requires that these connection points be physically secured and access to these areas is restricted. The access should be restricted to only those individuals (ideally as few as possible) with a business need.

9.2 *Develop procedures to help all personnel easily distinguish between employees and visitors, especially in areas where cardholder data is accessible.*

"Employee" refers to full-time and part-time employees, temporary employees and personnel, and consultants who are "resident" on the entity's site. A "visitor" is defined as a vendor, guest of an employee, service personnel, or anyone who needs to enter the facility for a short duration, usually not more than one day.

It is expected that in the normal course of business, organizations will have a variety of visitors at their facilities. However, since visitors may pose an increased security risk, their presence must be addressed differently than regular employees.

9.3 *Make sure all visitors are handled as follows:*

9.3.1 *Authorized before entering areas where cardholder data is processed or maintained.*

Your organization should limit access (only to employees required to have such access and that have also been properly authorized) to areas where cardholder data is processed or maintained. When circumstances require visitor access to areas where cardholder data is processed or maintained, then the visitor must properly be authorized prior to entering the restricted area. Depending on the organization's specific policies and procedures, this can be addressed in a variety of ways. At a minimum, the following elements must be considered when granting authorization to a visitor:

- Duration of visit
- Permissible level of access

- Purpose of visit
- Appropriate level of managerial awareness and sign-off

9.3.2 *Given a physical token (for example, a badge or access device) that expires and that identifies the visitors as non-employees.*

PCI DSS requirement 9.3.2 offers several benefits that allow strong visitor security controls. These benefits include having visitor access that can expire, ensuring visitors only have access for the time period authorized by the organization's management. Furthermore, a physical token allows easier identification of an individual's status. It will also permit quick identification of individuals who do not have authorized access to the cardholder data environment. In other words, if an individual is not an employee or an authorized visitor (as identified by a visitor token) then they have not been granted proper access to the area and they should not be allowed in the cardholder data environment.

9.3.3 *Asked to surrender the physical token before leaving the facility or at the date of expiration.*

This PCI DSS requirement ensures that the visitor's access token cannot be used maliciously or beyond the approved period of use. If the token is not promptly returned to the organization, an attacker can utilize the token and gain access to the cardholder data environment under false pretenses and without proper authorization.

9.4 *Use a visitor log to maintain a physical audit trail of visitor activity. Retain this log for a minimum of three months, unless otherwise restricted by law.*

The information that can be extracted from a visitor log is invaluable when investigating an incident. This is particularly true when it is used in conjunction with other physical security controls. For example, if during an investigation a surveillance camera shows a visitor entering a secure area at the time that a breach occurs, then the visitor log can be used to determine the identity of that visitor. Since many incidents may not be discovered in real time, a three-month retention period is required (unless otherwise restricted by law) for incident response and investigation purposes.

9.5 *Store media back-ups in a secure location, preferably in an off-site facility, such as an alternate or backup site, or a commercial storage facility.*

Compliance with PCI DSS requirement 9.5 offers two security benefits. One security benefit is directly related to physical security and the other is associated with the CIA Triangle that we discussed in Chapter 2.

Media backups contain invaluable data and information about the cardholder data environment and the organization. If they were not important, why would they be backed up? When these data sources are not properly secured, an attacker could obtain your organization's sensitive data. Going back to the CIA triangle availability is one of the key components. When organizations store backup media in a secure, offsite facility, they are taking some initial steps to an effective business continuity/disaster recovery plan and ensuring the availability of backup media containing cardholder related data.

9.6 *Physically secure all paper and electronic media (including computers, electronic media, networking and communications hardware, telecommunication lines, paper receipts, paper reports, and faxes) that contain cardholder data.*

Any media within an organization that contains cardholder data must be properly secured. PCI DSS requirement 9.6 includes media in both a paper and electronic format. By physically securing media containing cardholder data, the organization is likely to prevent unauthorized disclosure of sensitive information.

9.7 *Maintain strict control over the internal or external distribution of any kind of media that contains cardholder data including the following:*

9.7.1 *Classify the media so it can be identified as confidential.*

Although Chapter 2 discussed the overall importance of data classification to an organization's information security and data protection program, PCI DSS requirement 9.7.1 specifies media containing cardholder data be labeled as confidential. Clear identification of media as confidential alerts and reminds members of the organization that they must maintain strict control over the media and treat it in an appropriate and secure manner.

9.7.2 *Send the media by secured courier or other delivery method that can be accurately tracked.*

During the normal course of business operations, organizations may need to transport media containing cardholder data. This practice should be avoided as much as possible and only performed when required (organizations must carefully consider the risk-to-reward ratio of such activity when determining if this is a true requirement) to support critical business operations.

When the decision is made to transport the media, it must be done so by a secured courier or other delivery method that can be accurately tracked. This tracking capability enables the organization to monitor their data when it is not in their immediate possession. This tracking information can also be used to support a data breach or security investigation.

9.8 *Ensure management approves any and all media that is moved from a secured area (especially when media is distributed to individuals).*

This is an administrative safeguard that allows management to be actively involved in any removal of media from a secured area and acts as a deterrent to anyone who believes they can remove cardholder data media from a secure area without being noticed. This control also offers positive confirmation that management has explicitly approved the removal of sensitive media from a secure area.

9.9 *Maintain strict control over the storage and accessibility of media that contains cardholder data.*

PCI DSS requirement 9.9 requires organizations to strictly control the storage and accessibility of media containing cardholder data. This control increases organizational accountability by ensuring strict management of how media containing cardholder data is stored and how access to that storage is granted. Without tight controls over the storage environment and the list of people who can access the storage environment, organizations will not be in a position to adequately protect stored media.

9.9.1 *Properly inventory all media and make sure it is securely stored.*

An accurate inventory allows for organizations to be accountable for media containing cardholder data at all times. Without having an accurate count of media, it is impossible to know where it is and ensure that it has been properly secured.

The exact format of an organization's inventory of media containing cardholder data will vary from organization to organization, but at a minimum it should include the following information:

- Media type
- Date of original storage
- Information regarding removal from secure storage:
    - Date of removal
    - Purpose of removal
    - Confirmation/authorization by data custodian verifying media removal
    - Person removing media
    - Duration of media removal
    - Date of media return
    - Person returning media to secure storage
    - Confirmation from media custodian that media has been returned to secure storage

■ Information regarding media removal from secure storage
  ■ Reason for media disposal
  ■ Date of media disposal
  ■ Confirmation/authorization of media disposal from data custodian
  ■ Person disposing of media

9.10 *Destroy media containing cardholder data when it is no longer needed for business or legal reasons as follows:*

9.10.1 *Cross-cut shred, incinerate, or pulp hardcopy materials.*

Compliance with PCI DSS requirement 9.10.1 confirms that hardcopy materials are properly destroyed. The specific destruction methods listed (cross-cut shred, incinerate, or pulp) ensure that cardholder data cannot be read, deciphered, or otherwise recovered when destroyed. Less stringent hardcopy disposal methods (i.e., simply throwing away the material) increases the likelihood that cardholder data stored in hardcopy format will be compromised.

9.10.2 *Purge, degauss, shred, or otherwise destroy electronic media so that cardholder data cannot be reconstructed.*

PCI DSS requirement 9.10.2 is intended to accomplish the same cardholder data protection as requirement 9.10.1, with the difference that it applies to cardholder data stored in electronic media. Again, specific data-destruction methods (purging, degaussing, shredding, or otherwise destroying electronic media so that cardholder data cannot be reconstructed) are required to ensure that cardholder data cannot be viewed.

CHAPTER 7

Regularly Monitor and Test Networks

Regularly monitoring and testing all cardholder data networks within an organization is essential to keeping cardholder data secure and complying with Payment Card Industry Data Security Standards (PCI DSS). Having strong monitoring and testing practices will increase the overall security posture of an organization's cardholder data environment. By regularly testing critical network components within the cardholder data environment, organizations will be able to identify and correct any vulnerabilities before they are exploited by a malicious attack. Active monitoring will promptly alert an organization to any vulnerabilities within its networks. A timely and appropriate response will enable an organization to immediately address any issues, thereby mitigating the risk of an attacker compromising cardholder data.

This chapter discusses the PCI DSS requirements regarding the monitoring and testing of networks, including how the networks must be monitored and tested, how often they must be monitored and tested, and what kind of audit trails must be established in order to be PCI DSS compliant.

REQUIREMENT 10: TRACK AND MONITOR ALL ACCESS TO NETWORK RESOURCES AND CARDHOLDER DATA

Logging mechanisms and the ability to track user activities are critical. The presence of logs in all environments allows thorough tracking and analysis if something does go wrong. Determining the cause of a compromise is very difficult without system activity logs.

Logging is a critical component for PCI DSS requirement 10 as well as many other components of PCI DSS. Logging is an invaluable tool for identifying and tracking network activity associated with cardholder data. Due to the complexity of logging and the variations that can occur based on specific organizational needs, we will review the more common logging issues all organizations face. Additionally, we will discuss logging as it relates to specific PCI DSS compliance requirements. Organizations seeking further information can reference the Resources section of this book.

The following is from the National Institute of Standards and Technology's Special Publication 800-92, *Guide to Computer Security Log Management,* and provides a perspective on logs:

"A log is a record of the events occurring within an organization's systems and networks. Logs are composed of log entries; each entry contains information related to a specific event that has occurred within a system or network. Many logs within an organization contain records related to computer security. These computer security logs are generated by many sources, including security software, such as antivirus software, firewalls, and intrusion detection and prevention systems; operating systems on servers, workstations, and networking equipment; and applications."

10.1 *Establish a process for linking all access to system components (especially access done with administrative privileges such as root) to each individual user.*

Requirements 10.2.1 through 10.2.7 address the organization's need to implement automated audit trails with specified criteria that can then be utilized to determine and/or reconstruct events that occur on system components.

10.2 *Implement automated audit trails for all system components to reconstruct the following events:*

10.2.1 *All individual user accesses to cardholder data.*

Complying with this requirement provides the ability to trace all user access to cardholder data to a specific user. Without this mechanism in place, it is impossible to hold individuals accountable for their actions or determine which user performed a specific action.

10.2.2 *All actions taken by any individual with root or administrative privileges.*

This is very similar to the preceding requirement except that it focuses on root, or administrative, privileges. Since root, or administrative, privileges are the most powerful access roles, accurate logging of such powerful actions must be logged.

10.2.3 *Access to all audit trails.*

This type of logging can be valuable for determining who (and any associated actions the individual performed regarding audit trails) accessed audit trails. Malicious users will often attempt to alter audit trails in an attempt to hide any sign of their malicious or unauthorized activity.

10.2.4 *Invalid logical access attempts.*

An excessive number of invalid logical access attempts is often a telltale sign of a brute force attack or similar unauthorized attempt to gain access to a protected environment. Logging this information is a critical component in the investigation of an unauthorized attempt to access the cardholder data environment.

10.2 5 *Use of identification and authentication mechanisms.*

This type of logged information is useful for providing historical information regarding identification and authentication mechanisms. This type of information can be leveraged to show specific authentication and authorization decision criteria. Specifically, this data would show the detailed information of who attempted to access restricted information, resources, or transactions and was either successful or unsuccessful in doing so.

10.2.6 *Initialization of the audit logs.*

This requirement dictates that logs must accurately capture when an audit log was initialized. When the logging process begins, the information must be captured in the audit log in order to properly reconstruct the events being captured in the audit log.

10.2.7 *Creation and deletion of system-level objects.*

Requirement 10.2.7 aligns with 10.2 5. Although it does not provide information about identification and authorization, it does show what types of activities were performed (system-level object creation and deletion) by users who were properly identified and authenticated.

10.3 *Record at least the following audit trail entries for all system components for each event.*

When the information derived from the individual components of 10.3 is properly aggregated, it offers the details required for incident response and investigation. Exhibit 7.1 lists PCI DSS requirements 10.3.1 through 10.3.6 (which together make up the list of the audit trail entries that must be recorded) and a brief description of each component.

10.4 *Synchronize all critical system clocks and times.*

Although a seemingly obvious and simple requirement, it is critical to the overall validity and usefulness of a log. The accuracy of synchronized system clocks and times is required to validate the time and date associated with an event. For example, without synchronized clocks and accurate times, a user cannot accurately be tied to an event identified in the log. The accuracy of time and date reporting is also critical to the reliability of audit logs. These logs are used to validate the findings in an incident response investigation. Additionally, from a legal

PCI DSS Requirement	**Description**
10.3.1 *User identification*	The ID of the user associated with the event
10.3.2 *Type of event*	The act that the user ID was performing
10.3.3 *Date and time*	Exact date and time the event occurred
10.3.4 *Success or failure indication*	Indicates whether the attempted action was a success or failure
10.3.5 *Origination of event*	The source of the event
10.3.6 *Identity or name of affected data, system component, or resource*	Identifies the specific entity to which an action was performed

EXHIBIT 7.1   Specific Event-Logging Criteria

perspective, the accuracy of system clocks and times is an evidentiary requirement in criminal and civil proceedings.

10.5 *Secure audit trails so they cannot be altered.*

Since the accuracy of information listed in audit trails is required to validate the findings of an incident response investigation, the integrity of audit trails must also be protected. If audit trails are not maintained in a secure environment, then an attacker can easily manipulate the data in the audit trail in an attempt to hide their malicious behavior.

10.5.1 *Limit viewing of audit trails to those with a job-related need.*

This control falls under the concept of Least Privileged Access Control discussed in Chapter 2. Remember—the fewer the number of individuals accessing audit trails, the greater the level of security and data integrity of that audit trail. If an individual does not require access to audit trail information, as a requirement of their job, then there is no reason the individual should have access to the audit trail information.

10.5.2 *Protect audit trail files from unauthorized modifications.*

PCI DSS requirement 10.5.2 further supports the premise of protecting the integrity of audit trails. Organizations must implement protection mechanisms that ensure the security of the audit trail files by preventing unauthorized modifications.

10.5.3 *Promptly back-up audit trail files to a centralized log server or media that is difficult to alter.*

PCI DSS requirement 10.5.3 supports the mission of maintaining the integrity of audit trail files. This is accomplished in two steps. First, by mandating that audit trail files are promptly backed up, organizations increase the availability of the information and ensure there is another copy available for business continuity purposes. The second part of PCI DSS requirement 10.5.3 mandates storing the audit trail file in a centralized log server or media that is difficult to alter. When audit trail files are stored in a location/manner that is difficult to alter, it is less likely that the files will be altered. This is particularly true when they are stored in a centralized location. From an access control perspective, a centralized location is easier to manage and offers increased levels of audit-trail protection and integrity.

10.5.4 *Copy logs for wireless networks onto a log server on the internal LAN.*

PCI DSS requirement 10.5.4 addresses the concerns of wireless networks. Since wireless networks offer increased levels of risk to the cardholder data environment and its associated logs, this requirement mandates that a copy of the logs is moved from the wireless network onto a log server on the internal LAN.

10.5.5 *Use file integrity monitoring and change detection software on logs to ensure that existing log data cannot be changed without generating alerts (although new data being added should not cause an alert).*

This requirement mandates that an alert be generated when an audit trail is changed or deleted. This is done because any instance where information is changed or deleted from an audit log is typically indicative of inappropriate behavior and must be addressed immediately.

10.6 *Review logs for all system components at least daily. Log reviews must include those servers that perform security functions like intrusion detection system (IDS) and authentication, authorization, and accounting protocol (AAA) servers (for example, RADIUS).*

Note: Log harvesting, parsing, and alerting tools may be used to achieve compliance with requirement 10.6.

PCI DSS requirement 10.6 mandates that organizations review logs for all critical components of cardholder data systems on a daily basis. The requirement specifies that the reviews cover critical security-related systems such as IDS/IPS and remote access servers. The intent of daily review is to ensure that the review is conducted on a frequent enough basis to quickly identify and address any issues that are indicative of malicious activity.

10.7 *Retain audit trail history for at least one year, with a minimum of three months online availability.*

PCI DSS requirement 10.7 is in place to increase the value of audit trails. Remember, audit trails are critical components that enable organizations to identify, analyze, and otherwise investigate any abnormal activity within the cardholder data environment. The minimum duration of this requirement is one year, with three months of online availability. Unfortunately, many incidents are not discovered in real time, and often the integrity of the cardholder data environment has been compromised for a significant period of time prior to the organization's being alerted to an incident. Having detailed audit trail information for at least one year allows the incident response team to have a greater range of historical data. This information is critical for tracing the origins of an intrusion. The second part of the requirement (having three months of online availability) makes it possible for an investigation to proceed in a timely manner, which is critical to the investigation of compromised cardholder data environment.

REQUIREMENT 11: REGULARLY TEST SECURITY SYSTEMS AND PROCESSES

Vulnerabilities are being discovered continually by hackers and researchers, and being introduced by new software. Systems, processes, and custom software should be tested frequently to ensure security is maintained over time and with any changes in software.

Regularly testing the organization's security systems and processes is an essential part of validating that your organization is PCI DSS compliant. Although testing appears to be burdensome, it is the best way to validate PCI DSS compliance within your network. Not only does it confirm that you have the appropriate level of protection within your infrastructure, but it also acts as a fail-safe to make sure you have not missed any vulnerabilities during the completion of your routine information security practices and daily operations.

Your organization's required compliance level (as defined in Chapter 1) will determine what specific steps are required by the PCI DSS to test the organization's security systems and processes. However, there are many common best practices that should be incorporated at all levels of PCI DSS compliance.

Although many organizations may be required to have outside parties (scanning vendors or qualified security assessors) to aid in this process, it is recommended that organizations perform these tasks internally prior to an official assessment. The primary benefit that organizations will derive from this activity is that they will be in a position to identify any potential gaps in their PCI DSS compliance. This affords organizations the opportunity to proactively correct any gaps prior to non-compliance issues being discovered by an external assessor. Besides enjoying the distinct benefit of knowing where it stands before being told by an external assessor, the organization benefits from additional testing and validation cycles. Simply increasing the total number of assessments will increase the overall security posture of the organization, regardless of whether the assessments are internal or external. Furthermore, issues may arise in between assessments. Remember that assessments are point-in-time examinations and potential noncompliance issues may arise in between assessment periods.

It is also important to clarify some terms and definitions that commonly surface in testing security systems and processes. Otherwise confusion may occur, since the parties involved may be talking about the same thing but using different terminology.

Network scanning is a testing technique that relies on a port scanner to identify any hosts connected to your organization's network, the network services currently enabled by the hosts, and the associated application running the network service. It is important to note that a network scan will identify all active devices operating within the address space that was within the parameters of the network scan. However, it will not identify vulnerabilities.

A vulnerability scan must be conducted to ascertain specific vulnerabilities within the organization. This does not mean a network scan is not useful, but rather that different types of scans require different tools, each with a specialized function that should be utilized only for its intended purpose. In some regards, vulnerability scanning is similar to network scanning but offers additional information about specific vulnerabilities facing the organization. In addition to identifying hosts and open ports (like network scanning technologies), vulnerability scanners identify known flaws (out-of-date or unpatched software, known vulnerabilities or improperly configured software, and deviations from the organization's security policy).

NIST Special Publication 800-42, *Guideline on Network Security Testing,* defines penetration testing as:

> "Security testing in which evaluators attempt to circumvent the security features of a system based on their understanding of the system design and implementation."

The intent of such a test is to validate the security posture of the system and identify any weaknesses that are likely to be exploited by attackers. If the results of the test identify any weaknesses, the flaws can be corrected before they are exploited by malicious attacks.

In order for organizations seeking PCI compliance to get a comprehensive picture of their cardholder data environment, they need to perform penetration tests on both the network and application layers. Each layer presents its own unique security concerns, a fact that calls for separate tests.

It is important to note there are many different strategies, techniques, tactics, and tools that can be utilized to accomplish security testing. It is outside the scope of this text to specifically describe the art and skill of vulnerability scanning and penetration testing, although the Resources section provides information for those interested in furthering their knowledge of the topic.

11.1 *Test security controls, limitations, network connections, and restrictions annually to assure the ability to adequately identify and to stop any unauthorized access attempts. Use a wireless analyzer at least quarterly to identify all wireless devices in use.*

PCI DSS requirement 11.1 requires security controls, limitations, network connections, and restrictions to be tested annually. Annual testing ensures that the organization has the ability to adequately identify and stop any unauthorized access attempts. Since the wireless environment is inherently more risky than a wired environment, the use of a wireless analyzer is required on a quarterly basis to identify all wireless devices in use.

11.2 *Run internal and external network vulnerability scans at least quarterly and after any significant change in the network (such as new system component installations, changes in network topology, firewall rule modifications, product upgrades).*

Note: Quarterly external vulnerability scans must be performed by a scan vendor qualified by the payment card industry. Scans conducted after network changes may be performed by the company's internal staff.

PCI DSS requirement 11.2 states that internal and external network vulnerability scans are conducted at least once a quarter or after any significant change in the network. The first important note from this requirement is that the standard requires both internal and external scans. Both internal and external vulnerability scans must be performed because each of the vulnerability scans examines vulnerabilities from a different perspective.

The other important item to note from PCI DSS requirement 11.2 is that internal and external scans must be performed after any significant changes occur in the network environment. Any changes to system components, network topology, firewalls, or product upgrades can yield new vulnerabilities. Internal and external network vulnerability scanning will identify any new vulnerabilities so that they can be quickly remediated in order to maintain the integrity and security of the cardholder data environment.

11.3 *Perform penetration testing at least once a year and after any significant infrastructure or application upgrade or modification (such as an operating system upgrade, a sub-network added to the environment, or a web server added to the environment). These penetration tests must include [requirements 11.3.1 and 11.3.2.]*

PCI DSS requirement 11.3 is intended to address penetration testing requirements. At a minimum, organizations must perform testing on an annual basis, unless the organization has any significant infrastructure or application modification.

The standard requires a penetration test after any significant changes to the environment in order to validate that the change does not expose the cardholder data environment to any new or additional risk. The subcomponents of this requirement address the penetration testing at the network and application level.

11.3.1 *Network-layer penetration tests.*

Network-layer penetration is a proactive strategy to validate the strength of the organization's security posture at the network layer. This strategy (in conjunction with application-layer penetration testing) supports the defense-in-depth security methodology. Since potential vulnerabilities exist in both the network and application layers, penetration testing must occur at both levels in order to validate the effectiveness of the organization's information security and data protection strategy.

11.3.2 *Application-layer penetration tests.*

Similar in intent to network-layer penetration testing, application-layer penetration testing looks for any security deficiencies at the application layer. As mentioned in PCI DSS requirement 11.3.1, this works in conjunction with network-layer penetration tests to support the defense-in-depth security methodology.

11.4 *Use network intrusion detection systems, host-based intrusion detection systems, and intrusion prevention systems to monitor all network traffic and alert personnel to suspected compromises. Keep all intrusion detection and prevention engines up-to-date.*

PCI DSS requirement 11.4 mandates that organizations utilize network intrusion detection systems, host-based intrusion detection systems, and intrusion prevention systems to monitor all network traffic around the cardholder data environment. Recall from Chapter 2 that these technologies can be utilized to alert the organization to a potential breach in the cardholder data environment. Furthermore, the requirement states that the intrusion detection and prevention engines are properly maintained and kept up to date. Similar to antivirus definitions and engines, these components are critical to the proper functioning of these tools. In other words, intrusion detection and intrusion prevention technologies are only effective at identifying and preventing incidents based on the information stored in the engine. Hence, if the engine is not kept up to date, organizations run the risk of not being able to properly identify the latest threats.

11.5 *Deploy file integrity monitoring software to alert personnel to unauthorized modification of critical system or content files; and configure the software to perform critical file comparisons at least weekly. Critical files are not necessarily only those containing cardholder data. For file integrity monitoring purposes, critical files are usually those that do not regularly change, but the modification of which could indicate a system compromise or risk of compromise. File integrity monitoring products usually come pre-configured with critical files for the related operating system. Other critical files, such as those for custom applications, must be evaluated and defined by the entity (that is the merchant or service provider).*

Organizations seeking compliance with PCI DSS requirement 11.5 must implement file integrity–monitoring software to alert personnel to unauthorized modification of critical system or content files. The requirement also mandates that the file integrity–monitoring software be configured to perform critical file comparisons at least on a weekly basis. The intent of this standard is to ensure that organizations are alerted in a timely manner to any unauthorized modification of critical files located within the cardholder data environment. Conducting file comparisons on a weekly basis ensures that not too much time passes before an organization identifies a potential issue. Organizations must also recognize that PCI DSS requirement 11.5 includes an additional note regarding critical files. The note emphasizes that the definition of critical files is not restricted to those containing cardholder data. The definition is much broader in scope and includes files that do not regularly change, but unauthorized modification of such files would likely indicate a system compromise. Finally, the note indicates that most file integrity–monitoring software that is deployed comes preconfigured to monitor critical files related to the operating system. Organizations must individually evaluate and identify the critical files that are located in and associated with any in-house custom applications.

CHAPTER 8

Maintain an Information Security Policy

The foundation of an effective information security program is an information security policy. This living document captures the organization's strategic security objectives in a concise, organized, and documented format. The policy should also act as a broadly drawn roadmap for the organization's progress toward Payment Card Industry Data Security Standards (PCI DSS) compliance. A well developed policy is an invaluable tool that will assist employees in performing their daily operational tasks in accordance with the organization's required objectives. An effective policy also acts as a decision-making tool. Employees who make business decisions based on the organization's information security policy will likely choose alternatives that will add value and strengthen the organization's security posture. Without an information security policy to guide them, employees of an organization cannot be held accountable when it comes to compliance with the entity's information security program and protection of the cardholder data environment. In this chapter, we will discuss the importance of developing, maintaining, and distributing an information security policy and also highlight what the policy must contain in order to be PCI DSS complaint.

REQUIREMENT 12: MAINTAIN A POLICY THAT ADDRESSES INFORMATION SECURITY

A strong security policy sets the security tone for the whole company and informs employees what is expected of them. All employees should be aware of the sensitivity of data and their responsibilities for protecting it.

Although the Payment Card Industry Security Standards Council lists maintaining a policy that addresses information security as PCI DSS requirement 12, the last requirement of the PCI DSS, it does not mean that this is the least important requirement. As stated earlier, no single component is more important than any other component of PCI DSS compliance. The strength of the program comes from the sum of the required individual security controls acting in unison to offer a comprehensive security program that protects the cardholder data environment. Therefore, the design, implementation, and maintenance of an organization's information security policy are often at the foundation of a PCI DSS–compliant environment. It is best to think of the information security policy as a broadly drawn strategic roadmap that offers guidance to the organization. Unfortunately, many organizations develop a comprehensive information security policy and then move on. They incorrectly hold the perspective that the policy is a onetime task rather than a living process. In addition, many organizations fail to leverage their policy to effectively govern their information security program. Information security–policy management is a process, not a onetime event. It must be reflected by a living document in tune with the organization's current security posture. It is important that the policy be reviewed and updated regularly to ensure it is properly aligned with the current business environment and adequately reflects any significant changes to the organization's infrastructure. All too often, security policies are not regularly updated or an insufficient amount of time is spent during the update process to properly align the policy with the current state of the organization.

Developing a comprehensive policy upfront allows the organization to achieve PCI compliance in a more streamlined manner. This is not to say that the execution of PCI compliance is not important, but rather that a good information security policy will pave the way to PCI compliance. Now that we have an understanding of the importance of the information security policy, let us examine the specific components of PCI DSS requirement 12.

12.1 *Establish, publish, maintain, and disseminate a security policy that accomplishes the following:*

12.1.1 *Addresses all requirements in this specification.*

Obviously, it would not make much sense for an organization to develop and maintain security policies that were not in accordance with PCI compliance requirements. It is likely that a majority of organizations will have a security policy that not only includes compliance with PCI requirements but also contains components to address other types of regulatory compliance or addresses specific organizational requirements. Despite the fact that organizations may have multiple requirements, it is highly recommended that an organization have one comprehensive policy that incorporates PCI specific requirements and also organization-specific requirements. Organizations that develop and maintain only information security policies that are specific to PCI compliance will have a difficult time maintaining multiple policies, will risk having policies that do not properly align with business operations, and will likely incur additional costs.

12.1.2 *Includes an annual process that identifies threats and vulnerabilities, and results in a formal risk assessment.*

The intent of this standard is to ensure that organizations continually monitor their environments, develop a formal risk assessment, and implement tactical solutions to address any of the threats and vulnerabilities identified in the risk assessment process. Since the technology environment for many organizations is everchanging, new threats and vulnerabilities continually develop just as quickly as the ever-changing technology environment.

By having an annual review process built into the policy, there is a greater likelihood that the risk assessment is successfully completed in a timely manner and is properly aligned with the everchanging threat environment.

12.1.3 *Includes a review at least once a year and updates when the environment changes.*

PCI DSS requirement 12.1.3 mandates that organizations review their information security policy on an annual basis and perform updates of the policy when the cardholder data environment changes. Having a formalized review process conducted on an annual basis ensures that the organization is regularly reviewing and updating its information security policy as required. If there are any significant changes to the cardholder data environment that would impact the information security policy, then the organization must update the policy as soon as those changes to the cardholder data environment occur. Remember, the policy is a strategic working document that must accurately reflect the organization's current state and offer appropriate guidance for the overall protection of the cardholder data environment.

12.2 *Develop daily operational security procedures that are consistent with requirements in this specification (for example, user account maintenance procedures, and log review procedures).*

In order to effectively execute a strategic security initiative, operational security procedures must be developed and practiced on a regular basis. A policy can be viewed as a security strategy, and is a useful tool for achieving PCI compliance, only when it is properly executed. As PCI compliance is an ongoing and continuous process and not a onetime event, the appropriate security controls must be executed as part of daily operations rather than as a last minute add-on exercise. The best security results are achieved only when the processes are seamlessly integrated with daily business operational procedures. Effective information security and data protection strategies need to be executed in a manner that supports business objectives, not hinders them.

12.3 *Develop usage policies for critical employee-facing technologies (such as modems and wireless) to define proper use of these technologies for all employees and contractors. Ensure these usage policies require [requirements 12.3.1 through 12.3.10].*

PCI DSS requirement 12.3 focuses on "critical employee-facing technologies" because these are considered high-risk touch points. As with most policies, this is intended to educate employees on the appropriate use of such technologies. This increases end user accountability as well as clearly defining the organization's expectations and requirements. PCI DSS requirements 12.3.1 to 12.3.10 highlight the minimum requirements for becoming PCI compliant. However, depending on organization-specific needs, additional elements may be incorporated into the employee-facing usage policies.

12.3.1 *Explicit management approval.*

This element allows management to be aware of and ultimately approve the operational processes and procedures occurring within the organization. This is particularly important when dealing with high-risk areas such as employee-facing technologies. It is highly recommended that a formal process be implemented. This process should capture management's explicit approval as well as supporting documentation.

12.3.2 *Authentication for use of the technology.*

PCI DSS requirement 12.3.2 is considered a technical safeguard. It is required because proper authentication ensures that employees are who they claim to be and have been granted access rights to utilize employee-facing technologies. Without proper authentication, organizations cannot accurately verify the identity of the user requesting access to the cardholder data environment via employee-facing technologies.

12.3.3 *List of all such devices and personnel with access.*

An accurate inventory of assets and a supporting list of personnel authorized to access the devices is also an administrative control. This control allows organizations to quickly determine what devices are active and connected to the cardholder data environment and who in the organization can access the devices. This list should also be reviewed on a regular basis to ensure the least number of devices (required to support the business) and the fewest number of employees (access to the devices should only be granted to employees who require such access as part of their job) are connected to the cardholder data environment.

12.3.4 *Labeling of devices with owner, contact information, and purpose.*

This control aligns very closely with 12.3.3 and is designed as an administrative control to ensure that devices connected to the cardholder data environment are properly managed. Specifically, having the device owner, his contact information, and business purpose of the device allows organizations to better manage employee devices connected to the cardholder data environment. This information should also be reviewed on a regular basis for accuracy, business need, and alignment with the organization's critical employee-facing technology usage policy.

12.3.5 *Acceptable uses of the technologies.*

This component of the critical employee-facing technology usage policy clarifies the organization's expectations regarding acceptable use of the technology within the organization and cardholder data environment. This is intended to clearly communicate the organization's expectations and hold its employees accountable to the organization's acceptable use requirements. This type of policy should address what the employee can and cannot use the technology for. Typically, this type of policy addresses the issue of business versus personal use of company owned assets. Depending on the organization, it may also address appropriate business use of the technology and specific operating procedures. For example, technology *x* might only be used within the trusted internal network, while technology *y* could be accessed outside of the internal network through a secure remote access technology.

12.3.6 *Acceptable network locations for the technologies.*

As previously discussed, a lot of PCI compliance is achieved by utilizing the defense-in-depth security methodology. Specifically, many information security and data protection controls are based on security-focused network architecture. Since employee-facing technologies are considered high risk, it is likely that it will only be acceptable to implement these technologies in specific areas of the network (those with enhanced security protections).

12.3.7 *List of company-approved products.*

With a predetermined list of company-approved products and devices, organizations are better equipped to control employee-facing technologies. No product or technology unapproved by management should ever interface with the cardholder data environment. Furthermore, organizations improve their security posture when a formalized process is developed for management to approve products and devices. This is best accomplished when the products have been evaluated and tested to ensure they properly integrate with the cardholder data environment and do not create any security vulnerabilities or performance issues within the organization's existing infrastructure.

12.3.8 *Automatic disconnect of modem sessions after a specific period of inactivity.*

This is a technical control used to ensure that unnecessary modem sessions are not inadvertently left open. Unnecessary and open communication sessions (those left active when not currently needed for a valid business purpose) create potential security risks and potential access points to the cardholder data environment. Intruders can use the open communication sessions to infiltrate the internal network.

12.3.9 *Activation of modems for vendors only when needed by vendors, with immediate deactivation after use.*

Requirement 12.3.9 parallels 12.3.8 in that modem connections should be activated only when, and for as long as, they are needed to accomplish an appropriate business purpose. Specifically, this requirement addresses the security risks associated with vendors' access to the cardholder data environment. To help make sure vendors do not get excessive access, organizations can implement specialized processes and procedures. Typically, these programs should include formalized access request with:

- Vendor information
- Time and duration of access
- Date of access
- Business purpose
- Authorization and approval by the organization

12.3.10 *When accessing cardholder data remotely via modem, prohibition of storage of cardholder data onto local hard drives, floppy disks, or other external media. Prohibition of cut-and-paste and print functions during remote access.*

These are specific technical controls intended to address security concerns regarding cardholder data being transferred inappropriately during remote access sessions via a modem. Remember that PCI compliance requires a number of controls, configuration, and security-oriented implementations to protect and secure the cardholder environment. Local hard drives, floppy disks, and other external media often do not afford the same level of protection required by PCI. Cardholder data that is transferred or stored to such external devices places that data at extreme risk of loss, theft, or alteration. Therefore, specific measures must be taken to ensure that the cut-and-paste and print functions are disabled during remote access sessions.

Security is only as strong as its weakest link; careful consideration must be given to those end points of the cardholder environment that feature employee interaction. Many of these end points (local hard drives, floppy drives, and other external media) offer increased risk, so organizations must implement employee-interaction policies and procedures to ensure that these potential threat points are not exploited. PCI DSS compliance requires, at a minimum, that the policies address the following components described in requirements 12.3.1 through 12.3.10.

12.4 *Ensure that the security policy and procedures clearly define information security responsibilities for all employees and contractors.*

The primary strength of an information security policy is the ability to clearly define roles and responsibilities and to communicate expectations to employees and contractors. If an information security policy does not effectively communicate the roles and responsibilities of employees and contractors, then it will be impossible to hold such individuals accountable for their role in protecting the organization's information-based assets.

12.5 *Assign to an individual or team the following information security management responsibilities:*

12.5.1 *Establish, document, and distribute security policies and procedures.*

To get results, security policies and procedures must be properly established, documented, and distributed. The importance of clear communications that are properly distributed cannot be overstated. An organization cannot expect to have security-minded employees unless it properly disseminates security expectations. Many organizations find this task is most effectively performed by making policies and procedures readily available to employees (i.e., a secured intranet site) and by continually reminding employees (i.e., quarterly email reminders) of existing policies and promptly notifying employees about any changes to existing policies or any implementation of new security policies and procedures.

12.5.2 *Monitor and analyze security alerts and information, and distribute to appropriate personnel.*

Since information technology (particularly information security–related components of technology) is constantly changing, organizations must proactively monitor and analyze security-related alerts and information and properly share such information to the appropriate personnel within the organization. Organizations can turn to a wide variety of resources when obtaining or analyzing security-relevant information. The more common types include:

- PCI Security Standards Council
- Professional associations
- Trade journals/media outlets
- Vendor alerts
- Industry analysts

For those seeking specific resources and additional information for the items listed above, see the Resources section of this text.

12.5.3 *Establish, document, and distribute security incident response and escalation procedures to ensure timely and effective handling of all situations.*

PCC DSS requirement 12.9 addresses the specific components of a PCI compliant incident response plan. Requirement 12.5.3 addresses the need for organizations to properly document and distribute incident response procedures. The proper distribution of incident response procedures ensures that personnel have the ability to reference guidelines that allow them to effectively respond to incidents in a timely manner and in accordance with organizational requirements.

12.5.4 *Administer user accounts, including additions, deletions, and modifications.*

User account administration can be one of the most challenging tasks PCI compliant organizations will face. However, it is one of the most critical requirements for protecting access to the cardholder data environment. Many organizations have security controls in place to protect the organization from unauthorized access attempts. However, poorly managed authorized access attempts may yield the same dreaded results as an unauthorized individual who maliciously accesses the cardholder data environment. In other words, user accounts that are not properly administered could cause as many problems as an intruder accessing the coveted cardholder data environment.

Organizations need to develop policies and operating procedures that support user account addition, deletion, and modification. These policies and procedures must be carried out in an appropriate manner and under PCI compliant organizational requirements.

12.5.5 *Monitor and control all access to data.*

This control has two key components that must be followed in order to ensure protection of the cardholder data environment. The two key words are *monitor* and *control*. These two activities work in conjunction to manage and protect access to cardholder data. First, access to cardholder data must be restricted with a variety of controls (technical, administrative, etc.) in a manner that enforces the concepts of least privilege and data classification. These mechanisms can be viewed as the proactive strategies used to limit access and will likely prevent control problems from occurring in the first place. Monitoring activities are usually secondary, detective controls (although real-time monitoring and alert technologies can be deployed) to support access controls that have already been implemented. They can be described as the enforcement arm of controlling access to cardholder data. Monitoring can be used to alert organizations to any abnormal activity regarding access to sensitive cardholder data.

12.6 *Implement a formal security awareness program to make all employees aware of the importance of cardholder data security.*

A formal security awareness program is essential to ensuring all employees are properly made aware of their security roles and responsibilities within the organization. A formalized program develops a security-minded culture and enables employees to perform their jobs with security as a priority, not an afterthought.

12.6.1 *Educate employees upon hire and at least annually (e.g., by letters, posters, memos, meetings, and promotions).*

PCI requirement 12.6.1 takes a two-pronged approach to security awareness and education. First, employees joining the organization are educated into full security awareness. This is an excellent opportunity to set company expectations and requirements, and to get employees thinking about their security roles and responsibilities from day one. The second part of the approach is to continually remind and educate employees concerning these roles and responsibilities. The more frequent the reiteration of security fundamentals, the stronger the program. PCI compliance requires conducting an awareness program at least once a year, and more often is certainly better.

12.6.2 *Require employees to acknowledge in writing that they have read and understood the company's security policy and procedures.*

Similar to PCI DSS requirement 12.4, requiring employees to acknowledge and understand the company's information security policy and procedures provides clear communication and expectations for the individual. A written confirmation is a powerful aid in holding employees accountable for the organization's information security policies and procedures.

12.7 *Screen potential employees to minimize the risk of attacks from internal sources. For those employees such as store cashiers who only have access to one card number at a time when facilitating a transaction, this requirement is a recommendation only.*

Hiring the wrong person can be disastrous for an organization's PCI compliance strategy. Specifically, hiring an individual with an unsavory past for a high-trust position with access to valuable information is likely to lead to a variety of problems for an organization trying to achieve and maintain PCI compliance. A thorough background check, one including the person's criminal, financial, educational, and employment history, will allow management to determine whether or not they are selecting high-risk employees for sensitive positions.

12.8 *If cardholder data is shared with service providers, then contractually [requirements 12.8.1 and 12.8.2] are required:*

12.8.1 *Service providers must adhere to the PCI DSS requirements.*

In order for organizations to maintain adequate levels of protection over cardholder data, PCI DSS requirement 12.8.1 requires organizations to be accountable for sensitive cardholder data even if that data is shared with service providers. In other words, any service provider conducting business with an organization required to be PCI DSS compliant must also be compliant. It is up to the organization to confirm that any service provider it uses is PCI DSS compliant. Further details of these requirements are discussed in PCT DSS Appendix A which, in this book, is analyzed along with PCI DSS requirement 2.4 in Chapter 3.

12.8.2 *Agreement that includes an acknowledgement that the service provider is responsible for the security of cardholder data the provider possesses.*

The intent of requirement 12.8 is to offer your organization increased security and reduced liability when working with service providers. Requirements 12.8.1 and 12.8.2 offer a proactive approach to information security controls and risk management by clarifying expectations with the service provider before business transactions occur.

12.9 *Implement an incident response plan. Be prepared to respond immediately to a system breach.*

Unfortunately, organizations must face the fact that, no matter how strong their information security and risk management program, a system breach can still occur. Not responding in an appropriate manner will certainly make a bad situation worse.

One of the greatest challenges organizations face when managing a security breach is making decisions in a high pressure situation with limited time and less than ideal conditions. Adding to the difficulty is the multifaceted nature of security problems. The organization must address a variety of issues surrounding legal and compliance, technology, customer service, communications, and branding. Having a clearly defined plan ready and waiting allows the organization to make critical decisions at a stressful time. Organizations are likely to make the wrong decision if they cannot follow a plan developed in a less stressful environment. If there is a breach, a prepared organization can focus on responding and not on deciding how to respond. The time saved may be crucial when invaluable information regarding the breach is about to be lost.

12.9.1 *Create the incident response plan to be implemented in the event of system compromise. Ensure the plan addresses, at a minimum, specific incident response procedures, business recovery and continuity procedures, data backup processes, roles and responsibilities, and communication and contact strategies (for example, informing the Acquirers and credit card associations)*

Chapter 2 of this text discusses the key components of incident response and the critical components that organizations must consider when designing, implementing, and managing their incident response programs. The following information will highlight the role of incident response as part of the organization's overall compliance with the PCI DSS.

PCI DSS requirement 12.9.1 mandates that an incident response plan be implemented in the event of a system compromise. Furthermore, this requirement continues its mission by requiring that the plan addresses incident response procedures, business recovery and continuity procedures, data backup processes, roles and responsibilities, and communication strategies. It is highly recommended that this plan have full management support and that it be developed by a team of the organization's subject matter experts (representing each of the areas required to be addressed by PCI DSS 12.9.1). Additionally, this plan should be regularly reviewed, updated, and tested to ensure the plan accurately reflects the organization's current incident response capabilities and ensures that the organization can respond according to plan in the event of a system compromise.

12.9.2 *Test the plan at least annually.*

By testing the incident response plan annually, the organization can remain confident of responding appropriately to any incident or data breach, and of keeping the organization's plans up to date so it can respond to an incident in the current technology environment.

12.9.3 *Designate specific personnel to be available on a 24/7 basis to respond to alerts.*

By nature, incidents are unplanned events that must be responded to in a timely and appropriate manner. Therefore, having personnel with the ability to respond on a 24/7 basis is essential. Organizations must respond in real time, and they must do so with the right personnel. The "right people" are those who have been properly trained to respond in accordance with your organization's incident response procedures.

12.9.4 *Provide appropriate training to staff with security breach response responsibilities.*

The individuals who have been designated to respond to a security breach must be properly trained. In addition to being trained with organization-specific security breach policies and procedures, they should be trained in industry-approved forensic methodologies, tools, and best practices. Even armed with the best intentions, an individual who is not properly trained in the intricacies of computer forensics can quickly damage invaluable evidence used in a forensic investigation or in civil or criminal proceedings. Unfortunately, the volatile nature of the electronic evidence makes it very easy for an unqualified individual to damage evidence beyond a recoverable state. See the Resources section for detailed information regarding computer forensics.

12.9.5 *Include alerts from intrusion detection, intrusion prevention, and file integrity monitoring systems.*

Proactive security monitoring tools (intrusion detection, intrusion prevention, and file integrity monitoring) have alert mechanisms intended to notify system administrators and incident response teams of abnormal system activity. These tools must be configured to alert designated personnel in a timely manner so that an organization can carry out incident response in an appropriate manner.

12.9.6 *Develop process to modify and evolve the incident response plan according to lessons learned and to incorporate industry developments.*

Since the incident response cycle is a fluid and continuous process, it must adjust to internal and external influences (organizational and technical changes, newly identified threats and vulnerabilities, and industry trends) in an appropriate and timely fashion. In order for organizations to maintain this level of adaptability, they must constantly modify their incident response plans. This is best accomplished by using lessons learned and industry developments as trigger events based on newly identified internal and external impacts. Lessons learned can be leveraged after an actual event, planned testing, or training event. This is a great question-based methodology for analyzing and assessing your organization's incident response capabilities. The following is a sample of some of the basic and more common questions organizations should ask:

- What could we have done differently?
- Did we meet the objectives stated in our plan?
- What do we need to change to be more successful in the future?
- Do we have adequate resources (budget/staff) to succeed?

Staying abreast of industry trends can also provide strong indicators of when an incident response plan needs updating.

PCI DSS requirement 12.10 is intended to ensure there are no unsecured or unmanaged connections. Unknown or unmanaged connections are the gateway to the cardholder data environment that malicious attackers are looking for. Requirements 12.10.1 through 12.10.4 describe the specific security controls that organizations are required to implement in order to properly manage connected entities in a secure manner.

12.10 *All processors and service providers must maintain and implement policies and procedures to manage connected entities, to include [requirements 12.10.1 through 12.10.4].*

12.10.1. *Maintain a list of connected entities.*

This control is used to identify and manage all of the active connected entities. This list needs to be proactively managed and regularly updated to ensure its accuracy and overall effectiveness.

12.10.2. *Ensure proper due diligence is conducted prior to connecting an entity.*

Proper due diligence is an excellent security control. It allows organizations to gather and verify information about a connecting entity before authorizing a connection to the cardholder data environment. Due diligence is a proactive strategy that enables organizations to validate they are connecting and transacting with the types of service providers that live up to the organization's requirements and standards.

12.10.3. *Ensure the entity is PCI DSS compliant.*

This is relatively straightforward. It is important to ensure that the connected entity meets PCI DSS compliance requirements. It is recommended that this be accomplished by means of an objective third-party audit and managed on an ongoing basis through contractual requirements including "right to audit" or similar controls.

12.10.4. *Connect and disconnect entities by following an established process.*

PCI DSS requirement 12.10.4 is similar in nature and offers some benefits gained by effective change control. By having formalized procedures that authorize, control, and otherwise manage the connection and disconnection of entities, an organization significantly strengthens the overall strength the control environment. These formalized procedures will ensure that connections occur only under controlled circumstances (and in accordance with the criteria of PCI DSS requirement 12.10) and that entities are promptly disconnected when the entity no longer requires connection to the cardholder data environment.

PART 3

Strategy and Operations

Vision without action is a daydream; action without vision is a nightmare.

Japanese Proverb

CHAPTER 9

Assessment and Remediation

There are three primary assessment tools associated with Payment Card Industry Data Security Standards (PCI DSS) that organizations can utilize to achieve PCI DSS compliance. Depending on the organization's specific merchant or service provider status, these assessment methodologies may be optional or required. Where applicable, it is recommended that organizations leverage as many of these resources for PCI DSS compliance as possible. The following information is offered so organizations can be made aware of the resources available to them and also have an overview of each of these assessment methodologies. Organizations are encouraged to see the Resources section of this text as well and to regularly consult the Supporting Documents section at the Web site of the PCI Security Standards Council for updates.

PCI DSS PAYMENT CARD INDUSTRY SELF-ASSESSMENT QUESTIONNAIRE

The PCI Self-Assessment Questionnaire (SAQ) is an important validation tool that is primarily used by smaller merchants and service providers to demonstrate PCI DSS compliance. The currently posted version of the SAQ is based on the PC DSS from January 2005, and it will be valid until version 1.1 of the SAQ is released.

PCI DSS SECURITY AUDIT PROCEDURES

This document is designed for use by assessors who are conducting onsite reviews for merchants, and for service providers required to validate compliance with PCI DSS requirements. The requirements and audit procedures presented in this document are based on the PCI DSS.

PCI DSS SECURITY SCANNING PROCEDURES

This document explains the purpose and scope of the PCI security scan for merchants and service providers who undergo PCI security scans to help validate compliance with the PCI DSS. Approved scanning vendors also use this document to assist merchants and service providers in determining the scope of the PCI security scan.

LEVERAGING SELF-ASSESSMENT

Even if your organization will be relying on external resources for PCI DSS–related compliance initiatives, it is highly recommended to leverage self-assessment tools. The most significant benefit of self-assessment is having the ability to know the compliance status of your organization's cardholder data environment before a third-party assessment. Self-assessment can also be used to assess and maintain PCI DSS compliance between third-party assessment cycles. Remember, your organization is responsible for continually protecting cardholder data, not just for passing third-party assessments.

Depending on your organization's information security posture, PCI DSS compliance can be overwhelming at first glance. In order to get your hands around the project and move your organization forward with its compliance initiatives, you must first perform a gap analysis and assessment to determine where you are, where you need to be, and how you are going to get there. The first step is to obtain appropriate management support.

STRATEGY AND PROGRAM DEVELOPMENT

Strategy and program development are probably the most critical phases of the cardholder data protection and PCI DSS–compliance program. These are the foundational steps in which the organization determines how it will address data protection and PCI DSS issues and who will ultimately be responsible for carrying out the compliance activities. It is critical to identify program objectives, players, and the methods by which objectives will be met. This is also the time to secure appropriate levels of executive support, as enterprise-wide data protection and cardholder programs are most successful when they have strong executive backing. This support is critical throughout the PCI DSS–compliance life cycle. The PCI DSS–compliance initiative's executive champion will be instrumental in securing appropriate resources during the program life cycle.

The next step is to designate a hands-on cardholder data–protection and PCI DSS–compliance team lead. Depending on organizational structure, this role is likely to be managed by a chief security officer, chief information officer, or general counsel. It is essential that the team lead be a person who is familiar with the systems used by the organization, the data stored in these systems, and the information security policies and procedures that exist within the organization. Finally, this individual must be able to keep abreast of changing trends and new government regulations.

The data protection and privacy team lead will have the following responsibilities:

- Building and managing a team of subject matter experts
- Acting as a liaison with the executive sponsor for PCI DSS–compliance initiatives
- Conducting general project management and oversight
- Maintaining and carrying out the organization's PCI DSS–compliance vision

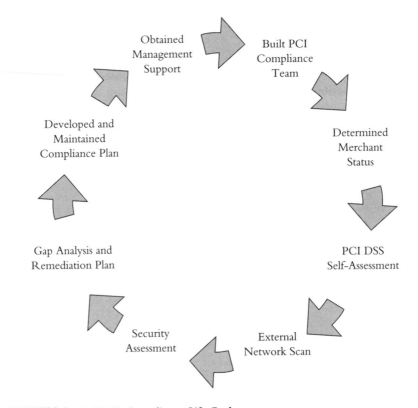

EXHIBIT 9.1   PCI DSS–Compliance Life Cycle

After obtaining the appropriate level of management support and building the team, the next step is to determine your merchant status/ level. This is based on the criteria found in Exhibit 1.7.

Exhibit 9.1 gives a pictorial view of the assessment and remediation cycle. It's pictured as a cycle to make the point that it is an ongoing process and not simply something that is completed only one time.

CHAPTER 10

PCI Program Management

In order to successfully maintain the enthusiasm and gains after the initial implementation of a Payment Card Industry Data Security Standard (PCI DSS) initiative, the organization must continually review its program, properly allocate resources, and conduct ongoing compliance analysis. The effective use of metrics enables the organization to objectively gauge the success of its program. Note that the use of metrics is more important than the type of metric selected by the organization. A detailed discussion of metrics is outside the scope of this book, but the main point is that the organization needs to establish baseline goals and objectives and measure progress against these goals and objectives. See the "Metrics" section in Chapter 2 for some possible metrics frameworks that your organization can implement to assist in PCI DSS compliance. The percent-effective metric is easy to implement and relatively easy to use, and it is highly effective. It helps monitor progress and can identify any gaps between actual performance and planned objectives. For example, if an organization determines that it is currently 50 percent compliant with the PCI DSS standards, 50 percent would be set as a baseline. The organization would set a goal to be 100 percent compliant by year-end and would evaluate its progress throughout the year by completing self-audits, compliance checks, and analysis to calculate its improvement results.

The self-audit concept is another valuable exercise for validating an organization's level of compliance with the PCI DSS standard. After implementing PCI DSS–program protections, it is a good time to test the waters and determine if there are there any remaining gaps between the PCI DSS requirements and the organization's daily operations. PCI DSS–compliance leaders need to ask questions to make sure they are taking their compliance activities in the right direction. Some of the questions that might be asked include:

- Is the organization as good as it says it is?
- Is the organization compliant with the relevant regulations enterprise wide or only in one business unit?
- Has the organization achieved compliance by aligning with other business objectives?
- Are there any practices that can be simplified, automated, or otherwise made more efficient?
- Is there anything else that can be done to add value to the organization?

An objective self-audit allows the organization to answer these questions and direct its PCI DSS–compliance activities in an appropriate manner.

CASE FOR STRATEGIC COMPLIANCE

Most organizations trying to become PCI compliant are likely to face other compliance requirements as well. Although each organization will have unique requirements to comply with (based on organizational structure, size, and specific industry requirements), entities that leverage a centralized compliance framework will achieve the greatest overall success with the lowest cost and greatest efficiency.

Many of the most common requirements regarding information security compliance are similar in nature. A well-organized and thought out compliance plan can often contain reusable components. Furthermore, many organizations are already compliant with many of the PCI DSS requirements because of the organizations' existing information security programs and simply need to make minor changes, or document existing policy and procedures in accordance with PCI DSS requirements. It is recommended that organizations seeking compliance perform a gap analysis—that is, compare their current information security program with PCI DSS requirements, then develop a strategic roadmap or action plan to remediate any inconsistencies. Exhibit 10.1 is a broadly framed example that can be modified to suit your organization's specific needs.

Phase	Tasks
PCI DSS Requirements Analysis	• Understand PCI DSS requirements and associated specific organizational impact
Cardholder Data Environment Analysis	• Identify which applications, systems, and network components within the organization must comply with PCI DSS
Prior Assessment Review	• Leverage any previous assessments related to cardholder data environment (audits, other compliance programs, etc.)
PCI DSS Gap Analysis	• Determine the organization's current level of PCI DSS compliance by completing the PCI DSS Self-Assessment Questionnaire
Project Plan	• Complete detailed project plan in accordance with findings in the PCI DSS Gap Analysis
Post-Project Review/PCI DSS Program Management	• Proactively manage PCI DSS compliance and begin preparation for annual audit and compliance validation

EXHIBIT 10.1   PCI Compliance Strategic Roadmap

WHO SHOULD BE INVOLVED ACHIEVING PCI DSS COMPLIANCE FOR OUR ORGANIZATION?

At first, this appears to be a straightforward question with seemingly easy answers. However, depending on your organization, the answer can be relatively complex. Beyond the obvious influences on the answer (organization size and structure, volume of transactions, business model, etc.), the answer really comes down to "it depends." Remembering that compliance with PCI DDS is the primary goal, getting there is more important than choosing the one perfect way of getting there. Thus, the suggestions in Exhibit 10.2 should be customized to fit your organization's specific needs and current maturity level regarding PCI DSS compliance.

Depending on your organization's specific PCI DSS–compliance strategy, there is most likely a point where you will incorporate the help of outside resources to assist in your PCI DSS–compliance strategy. This may include hiring additional resources to focus on specific parts of the compliance project strategy, remediation of any noncompliant findings, the outsourcing of certain processes, and finally (depending on your merchant status/level) selecting qualified security assessors and approved scanning vendors. In terms of selecting qualified security assessors and approved scanning vendors, the PCI Security Standards Council has made your life easier by maintaining a list of approved vendors (who have undergone a rigorous qualification process). However, your organization will still need to select a PCI Security Standards Council–approved vendor that suits your organization's specific needs. Although vendor selection and management are outside the scope of this book, it is important to discuss a few critical factors that will aid the success of your organization's PCI compliance initiative:

- Set clear objectives and strategies that can be properly communicated to the incoming vendor.
- Conduct due diligence to verify that the selected vendor will appropriately and adequately address your organization's needs.

Role	Description	Responsibilities
PCI DSS–Compliance Lead	• General knowledge of the organization's systems, data, and policies • Ability to identify experts within the organization to contribute to the policy	• Build and manage team • Communicate with executive sponsor • Perform general project management • Maintain and carry out the vision
Data Subject Matter Experts	• Intimate knowledge of the cardholder data environment requiring compliance with PCI DSS	• Identify and categorize the organization's data within the cardholder data environment • Work with the policy SME to determine what data is governed by PCI DSS
Systems Subject Matter Experts	• Intimate knowledge of the cardholder data environment requiring compliance with PCI DSS • Knowledge of how the systems are currently protected (firewalls, VPN, etc.)	• Document what measures are currently taken to protect the systems and the data stored in them • Identify extra measures that must be taken to protect systems and data and to achieve/maintain compliance with the PCI DSS
Policy Subject Matter Experts	• Intimate knowledge of the policies currently in place for the organization. • Understanding of PCI DSS, data security best practices, and industry resources	• Develop/maintain the company's information security policy based on recommendations made by the data and systems SMEs and in accordance with PCI DSS requirement 12
Business Process Analyst	• Excellent documentation skills • Ability to identify and align PCI DSS requirements with organizational business processes and effectively communicate any require changes	• Works with all SMEs to document workflows and business processes

EXHIBIT 10.2 PCI DSS–Compliance Roles

- Establish processes, controls, and reporting mechanisms so that your organization can easily monitor the status of expected deliverables.
- Follow your organization's formalized vendor selection process. If your organization does not have such a process, it is recommended that you select appropriate representatives from your organization to take part in the vendor selection process. Typically, they would include people from legal, operations, technology, and any other group affected by PCI DSS.

PCI DSS GLOSSARY, ABBREVIATIONS, AND ACRONYMS*

AAA: Authentication, authorization, and accounting protocol

Accounting: Tracking of users' network resources

Access Control: Mechanisms that limit availability of information or information processing resources only to authorized persons or applications

Account Harvesting: Process of identifying existing user accounts based on trial and error. [Note: Providing excessive information in error messages can disclose enough to make it easier for an attacker to penetrate and "harvest" or compromise the system.]

Account Number: Payment card number (credit or debit) that identifies the issuer and the particular cardholder account. Also called Primary Account Number (PAN)

Acquirer: Bankcard association member that initiates and maintains relationships with merchants that accept payment cards

AES: Advanced encryption standard. Block cipher adopted by NIST in November 2001. Algorithm is specified in FIPS PUB 197

---

*Used with permission. "Payment Card Industry (PCI) Data Security Standard: Glossary, Abbreviations and Acronyms", the contemporaneous version of which is available at the following internet address: https://www.pcisecuritystandards .org/pdfs/pci_dss_glossary_v1-1.pdf.

ANSI: American National Standards Institute. Private, non-profit organization that administers and coordinates the U.S. voluntary standardization and conformity assessment system

Anti-Virus Program: Programs capable of detecting, removing, and protecting against various forms of malicious code or malware, including viruses, worms, Trojan horses, spyware, and adware

Application: Includes all purchased and custom software programs or groups of programs designed for end users, including both internal and external (web) applications

Approved Standards: Approved standards are standardized algorithms (like in ISO and ANSI) and well-known commercially available standards (like Blowfish) that meet the intent of strong cryptography. Examples of approved standards are AES (128 bits and higher), TDES (two or three independent keys), RSA (1024 bits) and ElGamal (1024 bits)

Asset: Information or information processing resources of an organization

Assessment Log: Chronological record of system activities. Provides a trail sufficient to permit reconstruction, review, and examination of sequence of environments and activities surrounding or leading to operation, procedure, or event in a transaction from inception to final results. Sometimes specifically referred to as security assessment trail

Authentication: Process of verifying identity of a subject or process

Authorization: Granting of access or other rights to a user, program, or process

Backup: Duplicate copy of data made for archiving purposes or for protecting against damage or loss

Cardholder: Customer to whom a card is issued or individual authorized to use the card

Cardholder Data: Full magnetic stripe or the PAN plus any of the following:

    Cardholder name
    Expiration date
    Service Code

Cardholder Data Environment: Area of computer system network that possesses cardholder data or sensitive authentication data and those systems and segments that directly attach or support cardholder processing, storage, or transmission. Adequate network segmentation, which isolates systems that store, process, or transmit cardholder data from those that do not, may reduce the scope of the cardholder data environment and thus the scope of the PCI assessment

Card Validation Value or Code: Data element on a card's magnetic stripe that uses secure cryptographic process to protect data integrity on the stripe, and reveals any alteration or counterfeiting. Referred to as CAV, CVC, CVV, or CSC depending on payment card brand. The following list provides the terms for each card brand:

CAV Card Authentication Value (JCB International payment cards)

CVC Card Validation Code (MasterCard payment cards)

CVV Card Verification Value (Visa Inc. Inc. and Discover payment cards)

CSC Card Security Code (American Express)

Note: The second type of card validation value or code is the three-digit value printed to the right of the credit card number in the signature panel area on the back of the card. For American Express cards, the code is a four-digit unembossed number printed above the card number on the face of all payment cards. The code is uniquely associated with each individual piece of plastic and ties the card account number to the plastic. The following provides an overview:

CID Card Identification Number (American Express and Discover payment cards)

CAV2 Card Authentication Value 2 (JCB International payment cards)

CVC2 Card Validation Code 2 (MasterCard payment cards)

CVV2 Card Verification Value 2 (Visa Inc. Inc. payment cards)

Compensating Controls: Compensating controls may be considered when an entity cannot meet a requirement explicitly as stated, due to legitimate technical or documented business constraints but has sufficiently mitigated the risk associated with the requirement through implementation of other controls. Compensating controls must 1) meet the intent and rigor of the original stated PCI DSS requirement; 2) repel a compromise attempt with similar force; 3) be "above and beyond" other PCI DSS requirements (not simply in compliance with other PCI DSS requirements); and 4) be commensurate with the additional risk imposed by not adhering to the PCI DSS requirement

CIS: Center for Internet Security. Non-profit enterprise with mission to help organizations reduce the risk of business and e-commerce disruptions resulting from inadequate technical security controls

Compromise: Intrusion into computer system where unauthorized disclosure, modification, or destruction of cardholder data is suspected

Console: Screen and keyboard which permits access and control of the server or mainframe computer in a networked environment

Consumer: Individual purchasing goods, services, or both

Cookies: String of data exchanged between a web server and a web browser to maintain a session. Cookies may contain user preferences and personal information

Cryptography: Discipline of mathematics and computer science concerned with information security and related issues, particularly encryption and authentication and such applications as access control. In computer and network security, a tool for access control and information confidentiality

Database: Structured format for organizing and maintaining easily retrieved information. Simple database examples are tables and spreadsheets

Data Base Administrator (DBA): Database Administrator. Individual responsible for managing and administering databases

DBA (Doing Business As): Compliance validation levels are based on transaction volume of a DBA or chain of stores (not of a corporation that owns several chains)

Default Accounts: System login account predefined in a manufactured system to permit initial access when system is first put into service

Default Password: Password on system administration or service accounts when system is shipped from the manufacturer; usually associated with default account. Default accounts and passwords are published and well known

DES: Data Encryption Standard (DES). Block cipher elected as the official Federal Information Processing Standard (FIPS) for the United States in 1976. Successor is the Advanced Encryption Standard (AES)

DMZ: Demilitarized zone. Network added between a private and a public network to provide additional layer of security

DNS: Domain name system or domain name server. System that stores information associated with domain names in a distributed database on networks, such as the Internet

DSS: Data Security Standard

Dual Control: Process of using two or more separate entities (usually persons) operating in concert to protect sensitive functions or information. Both entities are equally responsible for the physical protection of materials involved in vulnerable transactions. No single person is permitted to access or use the materials (for example, the cryptographic key). For manual key generation, conveyance, loading, storage, and retrieval, dual control requires dividing knowledge of the key among the entities. (See also split knowledge)

ECC: Elliptic curve cryptography. Approach to public-key cryptography based on elliptic curves over finite fields

Egress: Traffic exiting a network across a communications link and into the customer's network

Encryption: Process of converting information into an unintelligible form except to holders of a specific cryptographic key. Use of encryption protects information between the encryption process and the decryption process (the inverse of encryption) against unauthorized disclosure

FIPS: Federal Information Processing Standard

Firewall: Hardware, software, or both that protect resources of one network from intruders from other networks. Typically, an enterprise with an intranet that permits workers access to the wider Internet must have a firewall to prevent outsiders from accessing internal private data resources

FTP: File transfer protocol

GPRS: General Packet Radio Service. Mobile data service available to users of GSM mobile phones. Recognized for efficient use of limited bandwidth. Particularly suited for sending and receiving small bursts of data, such as e-mail and web browsing

GSM: Global System for Mobile Communications. Popular standard for mobile phones Ubiquity of GSM standard makes international roaming very common between mobile phone operators, enabling subscribers to use their phones in many parts of the world

Host: Main computer hardware on which computer software is resident

Hosting Provider: Offer various services to merchants and other service providers. Services range from simple to complex; from shared space on a server to a whole range of "shopping cart" options; from payment applications to connections to payment gateways and processors; and for hosting dedicated to just one customer per server

HTTP: Hypertext transfer protocol. Open-internet protocol to transfer or convey information on the World Wide Web

ID: Identity

IDS/IPS: Intrusion Detection System/ Intrusion Prevention System. Used to identify and alert on network or system intrusion attempts. Composed of sensors which generate security events; a console to monitor events and alerts and control the sensors; and a central engine that records events logged by the sensors in a database. Uses system of rules to generate alerts in response to security events detected. An IPS takes the additional step of blocking the attempted intrusion.

IETF: Internet Engineering Task Force. Large open international community of network designers, operators, vendors, and researchers concerned with evolution of Internet architecture and smooth operation of Internet. Open to any interested individual

Information Security: Protection of information to insure confidentiality, integrity, and availability

Information System: Discrete set of structured data resources organized for collection, processing, maintenance, use, sharing, dissemination, or disposition of information

Ingress: Traffic entering the network from across a communications link and the customer's network

Intrusion Detection Systems: See IDS

IP: Internet protocol. Network-layer protocol containing address information and some control information that enables packets to be routed. IP is the primary network-layer protocol in the Internet protocol suite

IP Address: Numeric code that uniquely identifies a particular computer on the Internet

IP Spoofing: Technique used by an intruder to gain unauthorized access to computers. Intruder sends deceptive messages to a computer with an IP address indicating that the message is coming from a trusted host

IPSEC: Internet Protocol Security (IPSEC). Standard for securing IP communications by encrypting and/or authenticating all IP packets. IPSEC provides security at the network layer

ISO: International Organization for Standardization. Non-governmental organization consisting of a network of the national standards institutes of over 150 countries, with one member per country and a central secretariat in Geneva, Switzerland that coordinates the system

ISO 8583: Established standard for communication between financial systems

Key: In cryptography, a key is an algorithmic value applied to unencrypted text to produce encrypted text. The length of the key generally determines how difficult it will be to decrypt the text in a given message

L2TP: Layer 2 tunneling protocol. Protocol used to support virtual private networks (VPNs)

LAN: Local area network. Computer network covering a small area, often a building or group of buildings

LPAR: Logical partition. Section of a disk which is not one of the primary partitions. Defined in a data block pointed to by the extended partition

MAC: Message authentication code

Magnetic Stripe Data (Track Data): Data encoded in the magnetic stripe used for authorization during transactions when the card is presented. Entities must not retain full magnetic stripe data subsequent to transaction authorization. Specifically, subsequent to authorization, service codes, discretionary data/Card Validation Value/CodeCVV, and proprietary reserved values must be purged; however, account number, expiration date, and name, and service code may be extracted and retained, if needed for business

Malware: Malicious software. Designed to infiltrate or damage a computer system, without the owner's knowledge or consent

Monitoring: Use of system that constantly oversees a computer network including for slow or failing systems and that notifies the user in case of outages or other alarms

NAT: Network address translation. Known as network masquerading or IP-masquerading. Change of an IP address used within one network to a different IP address known within another network

Network: Two or more computers connected together to share resources

Network Components: Include, but are not limited to firewalls, switches, routers, wireless access points, network appliances, and other security appliances

Network Security Scan: Automated tool that remotely checks merchant or service provider systems for vulnerabilities. Non-intrusive test involves probing external-facing systems based on external-facing IP addresses and reporting on services available to external network (that is, services available to the Internet). Scans identify vulnerabilities in operating systems, services, and devices that could be used by hackers to target the company's private network

NIST: National Institute of Standards and Technology. Non-regulatory federal agency within U.S. Commerce Department's Technology Administration. Mission is to promote U.S. innovation and industrial competitiveness by advancing measurement science, standards, and technology to enhance economic security and improve quality of life

Non Consumer Users: Any individual, excluding consumer customers, that accesses systems, including but not limited to employees, administrators, and third parties

NTP: Protocol for synchronizing the clocks of computer systems over packet-switched, variable-latency data networks

OWASP: Open Web Application Security Project

Payment Cardholder Environment: That part of the network that possesses cardholder data or sensitive authentication data

PAN: Primary Account Number is the payment card number (credit or debit) that identifies the issuer and the particular cardholder account. Also called Account Number

Password: A string of characters that serve as an authenticator of the user

Pad: Packet assembler/disassembler. Communication device that formats outgoing data and strips data out of incoming packets. In cryptography, the one-time PAD is an encryption algorithm with text combined with a random key or "pad" that is as long as the plaintext and used only once. Additionally, if key is truly random, never reused, and, kept secret, the one-time pad is unbreakable

PAT: Port address translation. Feature of a network address translation (NAT) device that translates transmission control protocol (TCP)

or user datagram protocol (UDP) connections made to a host and port on an outside network to a host and port on an inside network

Patch: Quick-repair job for piece of programming. During software product beta test or try-out period and after product formal release, problems are found. A patch is provided quickly to users

PCI: Payment Card Industry

Penetration: Successful act of bypassing security mechanisms and gaining access to computer system

Penetration Test: Security-oriented probing of computer system or network to seek out vulnerabilities that an attacker could exploit. Beyond probing for vulnerabilities, this testing may involve actual penetration attempts. The objective of a penetration test is to detect identify vulnerabilities and suggest security improvements

PIN: Personal identification number

Policy: Organization-wide rules governing acceptable use of computing resources, security practices, and guiding development of operational procedures

POS: Point of sale

Procedure: Descriptive narrative for a policy. Procedure is the "how to" for a policy and describes how the policy is to be implemented

Protocol: Agreed-upon method of communication used within networks. Specification that describes rules and procedures that computer products should follow to perform activities on a network

Public Network: Network established and operated by a telecommunications provider or recognized private company, for specific purpose of providing data transmission services for the public. Data must be encrypted during transmission over public networks as hackers easily and commonly intercept, modify, and/or divert data while in transit. Examples of public networks in scope of PCI DSS include the Internet, GPRS, and GSM.

PVV: PIN verification value. Encoded in magnetic stripe of payment card

RADIUS: Remote authentication and dial-in user service. Authentication and accounting system. Checks if information such as username and password that is passed to the RADIUS server is correct, and then authorizes access to the system

RFC: Request for comments

Re-Keying: Process of changing cryptographic keys to limit amount of data to be encrypted with the same key

Risk Analysis: Process that systematically identifies valuable system resources and threats; quantifies loss exposures (that is, loss potential) based on estimated frequencies and costs of occurrence; and (optionally) recommends how to allocate resources to countermeasures so as to minimize total exposure. Risk assessment

Router: Hardware or software that connects two or more networks. Functions as sorter and interpreter by looking at addresses and passing bits of information to proper destinations. Software routers are sometimes referred to as gateways

RSA: Algorithm for public-key encryption described in 1977 by Ron Rivest, Adi Shamir, and Len Adleman at Massachusetts Institute of Technology (MIT); letters RSA are the initials of their surnames

Sanitization: Process for deleting sensitive data from a file, device, or system; or for modifying data so that it is useless if accessed in an attack

SANS: SysAdmin, assessment, Network, Security Institute (See www.sans.org)

Security Officer: Primary responsible person for security related affairs of an organization

Security Policy: Set of laws, rules, and practices that regulate how an organization manages, protects, and distributes sensitive information

Sensitive Authentication Data: Security-related information (Card Validation Codes/Values complete track data, and PINs, and PIN Blocks) used to authenticate cardholders,) appearing in plaintext or otherwise unprotected form. Disclosure, modification, or destruction of this information could compromise the security of a cryptographic device, information system, or cardholder information or could be used in a fraudulent transaction

Separation of Duties: Practice of dividing steps in a function among different individuals, so as to keep a single individual from being able to subvert the process

Server: Computer that providers a service to other computers, such as processing communications, file storage, or accessing a printing facility. Servers include, but are not limited to web, database, authentication, DNS, mail, proxy, and NTP

Service Code: Three- or four-digit number on the magnetic-stripe that specifies acceptance requirements and limitations for a magnetic-stripe read transaction.

Service Provider: Business entity that is not a payment card brand member or a merchant directly involved in the processing, storage, transmission, and switching or transaction data and cardholder information or both. This also includes companies that provide services to merchants, services providers or members that control or could impact the security of cardholder data. Examples include managed service providers that provide managed firewalls, IDS and other services as well as hosting providers and other entities. Entities such as telecommunications companies that only provide communication links without access to the application layer of the communication link are excluded

SHA: Secure Hash Algorithm. A family or set of related cryptographic hash functions. SHA-1 is the most commonly used function. Use of unique salt value in the hashing function reduces the chances of a hashed value collision

SNMP: Simple Network Management Protocol. Supports monitoring of network-attached devices for any conditions that warrant administrative attention

Split Knowledge: Condition in which two or more entities separately have key components that individually convey no knowledge of the resultant cryptographic key

SQL: Structured (English) Query Language. Computer language used to create, modify, and retrieve data from relational database management systems

SQL Injection: Form of attack on database-driven web site. An attacker executes unauthorized SQL commands by taking advantage of insecure code on system connected to the Internet. SQL injection attacks are used to steal information from a database from which the data would normally not be available and/or to gain access to an organization's host computers through the computer that is hosting the database

SSH: Secure shell. Protocol suite providing encryption for network services like remote login or remote file transfer

SSID: Service set identifier. Name assigned to wireless WiFi or IEEE 802.11 network

SSL: Secure sockets layer. Established industry standard that encrypts the channel between a web browser and web server to ensure the privacy and reliability of data transmitted over this channel

Strong Cryptography: General term to indicate cryptography that is extremely resilient to cryptanalysis. That is, given the cryptographic method (algorithm or protocol), the cryptographic key or protected data is not exposed. The strength relies on the cryptographic key used. Effective size of the key should meet the minimum key size of comparable strengths recommendations. One reference for minimum comparable strength notion is NIST Special Publication 800-57, August, 2005 () or others that meet the following minimum comparable key bit security:

- 80 bits for secret key–based systems (for example TDES)
- 1024 bits modulus for public key algorithms based on the factorization (for example, RSA)

- 1024 bits for the discrete logarithm (for example, Diffie-Hellman) with a minimum 160 bits size of a large subgroup (for example, DSA)
- 160 bits for elliptic curve cryptography (for example, ECDSA)

System Components: Any network component, server, or application included in or connected to the cardholder data environment

TACACS: Terminal access controller access control system. Remote authentication protocol

Tamper-resistance: System that is difficult to modify or subvert, even for an assailant with physical access to the system

TCP: Transmission control protocol

TDES: Triple Data Encription Standard also known as 3DES. Block cipher formed from the DES cipher by using it three times

TELNET: Telephone network protocol. Typically used to provide user-oriented command line login sessions between hosts on the internet. Program originally designed to emulate a single terminal attached to the other computer

Threat: Condition that may cause information or information processing resources to be intentionally or accidentally lost, modified, exposed, made inaccessible, or otherwise affected to the detriment of the organization

TLS: Transport layer security. Designed with goal of providing data secrecy and data integrity between two communicating applications. TLS is successor of SSL

Token: Device that performs dynamic authentication

Transaction Data: Data related to electronic payment

Truncation: Practice of removing data segment. Commonly, when account numbers are truncated, the first 12 digits are deleted, leaving only the last 4 digits

Two-Factor Authentication: Authentication that requires users to produce two credentials to access a system. Credentials consist of something the user has in their possession (for example, smartcards or hardware tokens) and something they know—for example, a password). To access a system, the user must produce both factors

UDP: User datagram protocol

UserID: A character string used to uniquely identify each user of a system

Virus: Program or string of code that can replicate itself and cause modification or destruction of software or data

VPN: Virtual private network. Private network established over a public network

Vulnerability: Weakness in system security procedures, system design, implementation, or internal controls that could be exploited to violate system security policy

Vulnerability Scan: Scans used to identify vulnerabilities in operating systems, services, and devices that could be used by hackers to target the company's private network

WEP: Wired equivalent privacy. Protocol to prevent accidental eavesdropping and intended to provide comparable confidentiality to traditional wired network. Does not provide adequate security against intentional eavesdropping (for example, cryptanalysis)

WPA: WiFi Protected Access (WPA and WPA2). Security protocol for wireless (WiFi) networks. Created in response to several serious weaknesses in the WEP protocol

XSS: Cross-site scripting. Type of security vulnerability typically found in web applications. Can be used by an attacker to gain elevated privilege to sensitive page content, session cookies, and a variety of other objects

REFERENCES

American Bar Association. *International Guide to Privacy*. Chicago: ABA, 2004.

Bradley, Tony. *PCI Compliance: Understand and Implement Effective PCI Data Security Standard Compliance*. Burlington, MA: Syngress, 2008.

Cole, Eric, Ronald Krutz, and James W. Conley. *Network Security Bible*. Indianapolis: Wiley, 2005.

Harris, Shon. *CISSP All-in-One Exam Guide,* third ed. New York: McGraw-Hill/Osborne, 2005.

Jaquith, Andrew. *Security Metrics: Replacing Fear, Uncertainty, and Doubt*. Boston: Addison-Wesley, 2007.

Noonan, Wes, and Ido Dubrawsky. *Firewall Fundamentals: An Introduction to Network and Computer Firewall Security*. Indianapolis: Cisco Press, 2006.

Ponemon Institute, LLC. *2007 Annual Study: U.S. Cost of a Data Breach: Understanding Financial Impact, Customer Turnover, and Preventative Solutions*. (Available at www.ponemon.org)

Payment Card Industry

The PCI Security Standards Council
www.pcisecuritystandards.org

PCI DSS
www.pcisecuritystandards.org/tech/index.htm

PCI SSC New Self-Assessment Questionnaire (SAQ)
www.pcisecuritystandards.org/tech/saq.htm

PIN Entry Devices
www.pcisecuritystandards.org/pin

Qualified Security Assessors (QSAs)
www.pcisecuritystandards.org/resources/qualified_security_
assessors.htm

Approved Scanning Vendors (ASVs)
www.pcisecuritystandards.org/resources/approved_scanning_
vendors.htm

PCI DSS Supporting Documents
www.pcisecuritystandards.org/tech/supporting_documents.htm

Visa Cardholder Information Security Program
www.usa.visa.com/merchants/risk_management/cisp.
html?it=fl|/index.html|http://www.usa.visa.com/VisaHome
.swf|ev_merchriskmanage_click&rand=1002969

MasterCard
www.mastercard.com/us/merchant/security/index.html

American Express
>   https://www209.americanexpress.com/merchant/singlevoice/dsw/
>   FrontServlet?request_type=dsw&pg_nm=home&ln=en&frm=US

Discover
>   www.discovernetwork.com/resources/data/data_security.html

JCB International Credit Card Co., Ltd.
>   www.jcbusa.com

Security Professional Associations

The International Information Systems Security Certification Consortium (ISC)^2
>   www.isc2.org/cgi-bin/index.cgi

The Information Systems Audit and Control Association (ISACA)
>   www.isaca.org

The Association of Certified Fraud Examiners (ACFE)
>   www.acfe.com

The International Society of Forensic Computer Examiners (ISFCE)
>   www.certified-computer-examiner.com/index.html

ASIS International
>   www.asisonline.org

Incident Response

The CERT® Coordination Center (CERT/CC)
>   www.cert.org

The United States Computer Emergency Readiness Team (US-CERT)
>   www.us-cert.gov

Data Breach Notification Laws, State by State
>   www.csoonline.com/read/020108/ammap/ammap.html

Media Resources

SC Magazine
>   www.scmagazineus.com

CSO Magazine
www.csoonline.com

Training

The SANS™ Institute (SysAdmin, Audit, Network, Security)
www.sans.org

Computer Security Institute
www.gocsi.com

Portals

SecurityNewsPortal (SNP)
www.securitynewsportal.com

CCCure.org
www.cccure.org

Frameworks

The Committee of Sponsoring Organizations of the Treadway Commission (COSO)
www.coso.org

COBIT
www.isaca.org/Template.cfm?Section=COBIT6&Template=/TaggedPage/TaggedPageDisplay.cfm&TPLID=&ContentID=7981

National Institute of Standards and Technology (NIST)

NIST Special Publication 800-100: *Information Security Handbook: A Guide for Managers*
csrc.nist.gov/publications/nistpubs/800-100/SP800-100-Mar07-2007.pdf

NIST Special Publication 800-30: *Risk Management Guide for Information Technology Systems*
csrc.nist.gov/publications/nistpubs/800-30/sp800-30.pdf

NIST Special Publication 800-80 (DRAFT): *Guide for Developing Performance Metrics for Information Security*
csrc.nist.gov/publications/drafts/draft-sp800-80-ipd.pdf

NIST Special Publication 800-94: *Guide to Intrusion Detection and Prevention Systems (IDPS)*
csrc.nist.gov/publications/nistpubs/800-94/SP800-94.pdf

NIST Special Publication 800-97: *Establishing Wireless Robust Security Networks: A Guide to IEEE 802.11i*
csrc.nist.gov/publications/nistpubs/800-97/SP800-97.pdf

NIST Special Publication 800-113 (DRAFT): *Guide to SSL VPNs*
csrc.nist.gov/publications/drafts/SP800-113/Draft-SP800-113.pdf

NIST Special Publication 800-114: *User's Guide to Securing External Devices for Telework and Remote Access*
csrc.nist.gov/publications/nistpubs/800-114/SP800-114.pdf

NIST Special Publication 800-115 (DRAFT): *Technical Guide to Information Security Testing*
csrc.nist.gov/publications/PubsDrafts.html#SP-800-115

NIST Special Publication 800-97: *Establishing Wireless Robust Security Networks: A Guide to IEEE 802.11i*
csrc.nist.gov/publications/nistpubs/800-97/SP800-97.pdf

NIST Special Publication 800-111: *Guide to Storage Encryption Technologies for End User Devices*
csrc.nist.gov/publications/nistpubs/800-111/SP800-111.pdf

NIST Special Publication 800-92: *Guide to Computer Security Log Management*
csrc.nist.gov/publications/nistpubs/800-92/SP800-92.pdf

NIST Special Publication 800-95: *Guide to Secure Web Services*
csrc.nist.gov/publications/nistpubs/800-95/SP800-95.pdf

NIST Special Publication 800-70: *Security Configuration Checklists Program for IT Products—Guidance for Checklist Users and Developers*
csrc.nist.gov/checklists/docs/SP_800-70_20050526.pdf

NIST Special Publication 800-86: *Guide to Integrating Forensic Techniques into Incident Response*
csrc.nist.gov/publications/nistpubs/800-86/SP800-86.pdf

NIST Special Publication 800-113 (DRAFT): *Guide to SSL VPNs*
csrc.nist.gov/publications/drafts/SP800-113/Draft-SP800-113.pdf

NIST Special Publication 800-77: *Guide to IPsec VPNs*
csrc.nist.gov/publications/nistpubs/800-77/sp800-77.pdf

NIST Special Publication 800-65: *Integrating IT Security into the Capital Planning and Investment Control Process*
csrc.nist.gov/publications/nistpubs/800-65/SP-800-65-Final.pdf

NIST Special Publication 800-57: *Recommendation for Key Management—Part 1 (General)*
csrc.nist.gov/publications/nistpubs/800-57/sp800-57-Part1-revised2_Mar08-2007.pdf

NIST Special Publication 800-55 Rev 1(DRAFT): *Performance Measurement Guide for Information Security*
csrc.nist.gov/publications/drafts/800-55-rev1/Draft-SP800-55r1.pdf

NIST Special Publication 800-50: *Building an Information Technology Security Awareness and Training Program*
csrc.nist.gov/publications/nistpubs/800-50/NIST-SP800-50.pdf

NIST Special Publication 800-48 Rev1 (DRAFT): *Wireless Network Security for IEEE 802.11 a/b/g and Bluetooth*
csrc.nist.gov/publications/drafts/800-48-rev1/Draft-SP800-48r1.pdf

NIST Special Publication 800-42: *Guideline on Network Security Training*
csrc.nist.gov/publications/nistpubs/800-42/NIST-SP800-42.pdf

NIST Special Publication 800-40: *Creating a Patch and Vulnerability Management Program*
csrc.nist.gov/publications/nistpubs/800-40-Ver2/SP800-40v2.pdf

Open Web Application Security Project (OWASP)
www.owasp.org/index.php/Main_Page

ISO/IEC 27002:2005
www.iso.org/iso/iso_catalogue/catalogue_tc/catalogue_detail.htm?csnumber=50297

COBIT
www.isaca.org/Template.cfm?Section=COBIT6&Template=/TaggedPage/TaggedPageDisplay.cfm&TPLID=55&ContentID=31519

Metrics

Balanced Scorecard
www.balancedscorecard.org

SecurityMetrics.Org
www.securitymetrics.org/content/Wiki.jsp

Common Vulnerability Scoring System (CVSS-SIG)
www.first.org/cvss

Vulnerability Resources

National Vulnerability Database (NVD)
nvd.nist.gov/nvd.cfm

IBM Internet Security Systems (ISS)
xforce.iss.net/xforce/alerts

Qualys
www.qualys.com/research/alerts

Cisco
tools.cisco.com/MySDN/Intelligence/home.x

Tenable Network Security
www.nessus.org/plugins

Microsoft Security Process Map
www.microsoft.com/technet/security/map/default.mspx

Microsoft TechNet Security Center
www.microsoft.com/technet/security/default.mspx

SANS Top-20 Security Risks
www.sans.org/top20

INDEX